Praise for *You Are the One You've Been Waiting For*

"This profound and readable book provides clear guidelines for therapists and clients alike. In ways that complement my own work, clients learn how to unload the cultural and family burdens that block intimacy by keeping them locked in rigid gender roles. Therapists learn an empowering and practical process for treating couples. I enthusiastically recommend this book to anyone serious about improving relationships in the world today!"

TERRENCE REAL
author of *I Don't Want to Talk About It, How Can I Get Through to You?*, and *The New Rules of Marriage*

"This highly original book offers critical new insights into obstacles to the dance of intimacy. Most of us have inner exiled parts that carry burdens of shame and abandonment from our past. These interfere with our capacity for intimacy. Dick Schwartz shows us how to use the exiles our partners trigger in us to find and heal the source—our original attachment injuries. This releases our capacity to be fully alive in relationships."

BESSEL A. VAN DER KOLK, MD
medical director, the Trauma Center, and professor of psychiatry, Boston University School of Medicine

"*You Are the One You've Been Waiting For* is my relationship bible! The IFS principles and methods shared in this book have offered me direct access to 'courageous love' and a greater connection to my husband than I ever thought possible. The book is on my bedside table, and I turn to it as a nightly ritual."

GABBY BERNSTEIN
#1 *New York Times* bestselling author of *The Universe Has Your Back*

"Dr. Richard Schwartz's work on Internal Family Systems, along with his latest book, *You Are the One You've Been Waiting For*, has profoundly changed my life. One of life's most important endeavors is to learn how to have compassion for oneself, and his work has been instrumental in my own journey to do so. His unique approach has allowed me to grow with love and gentleness in all aspects of my being—cognitively, physically, and emotionally. I deeply believe his work will change the world. Dr. Schwartz's book is the number one tool I recommend for people who are seeking to find greater compassion and love for themselves and others, especially with regard to better understanding their role within the greater whole and world."

KRISTA WILLIAMS
cohost and founder of the top-rated *Almost 30* and *Morning Microdose* podcasts and founder of Making Tarot Modern

"*You Are the One You've Been Waiting For* convincingly reveals a profound truth: if we want to have deeply loving, authentic, meaningful intimate relationships we must begin with the one person we know we can influence—ourselves. Thoroughly researched yet totally accessible, Dr. Richard Schwartz's book is written in a compelling manner that had me hooked and gave me hope and tools for how I can enjoy more peaceful, courageously loving relationships."

TARA SCHUSTER
author of *Buy Yourself the F*cking Lilies* and the forthcoming *Glow in the F*cking Dark*

"In his new book, Richard Schwartz shares key insights for people who struggle to hold on to their sense of self in the context of relationships. *You Are the One You've Been Waiting For* is a must-read for anyone seeking a companion on the path toward self-compassion and love."

ESTHER PEREL
psychotherapist, author, and host of the *Where Should We Begin?* podcast

"Emerging research suggests that the Internal Family Systems model, developed by Dick Schwartz and outlined in this book, cultivates self-acceptance, enhances inner compassion, and improves emotion regulation skills. This book applies the IFS model to one of the most complex human challenges and opportunities for healing, which is navigating intimate relationships. Our modern culture leaves us adrift in a sea of misunderstandings about how to achieve and sustain intimacy, and this book guides the reader to realize that the healing journey must first start with oneself."

ZEV SCHUMAN-OLIVIER, MD
assistant professor, Department of Psychiatry, Harvard Medical School, and
director, Center for Mindfulness and Compassion, Cambridge Health Alliance

You Are the
One You've Been
Waiting For

ALSO BY RICHARD C. SCHWARTZ

No Bad Parts: Healing Trauma and Restoring Wholeness
with the Internal Family Systems Model

Introduction to Internal Family Systems

Internal Family Systems Therapy,
2nd edition (with Martha Sweezy)

Family Therapy: Concepts and Methods,
7th edition (with Michael P. Nichols)

The Mosaic Mind: Empowering the Tormented Selves of
Child Abuse Survivors (with Regina A. Goulding)

Metaframeworks: Transcending the Models of Family
Therapy (with Douglas C. Breunlin)

Handbook of Family Therapy Training and Supervision
(with Howard A. Liddle and Douglas C. Breunlin)

You
Are the
One

You've Been Waiting For

APPLYING
INTERNAL FAMILY
SYSTEMS TO
INTIMATE
RELATIONSHIPS

RICHARD C. SCHWARTZ, PhD

sounds true
BOULDER, COLORADO

Sounds True
Boulder, CO 80306

Published 2023

Previously published as *You Are the One You've Been Waiting For: Bringing Courageous
Love to Intimate Relationships*, 2008.

Cover and jacket design by Huma Ahktar
Book design by Charli Barnes

Printed in The United States of America

BK05811

Library of Congress Cataloging-in-Publication Data
Names: Schwartz, Richard C., author.
Title: You are the one you've been waiting for : applying internal family systems to
    intimate relationships / Richard C. Schwartz.
Description: Boulder, CO : Sounds True, 2023. | Earlier edition published: 2008. |
    Includes bibliographical references.
Identifiers: LCCN 2022035079 (print) | LCCN 2022035080 (ebook) | ISBN
    9781683643623 (paperback) | ISBN 9781683644231 (ebook)
Subjects: LCSH: Family psychotherapy. | Intimacy (Psychology) |
    Families--Psychological aspects.
Classification: LCC RC488.5 .S383 2023 (print) | LCC RC488.5
    (ebook) | DDC 616.89/156--dc23/eng/20220722
LC record available at https://lccn.loc.gov/2022035079
LC ebook record available at https://lccn.loc.gov/2022035080

Lovingly dedicated to my parents,
the late Gen and Ted Schwartz,
my biggest mentors and tor-mentors

Internal Family Systems Therapy

Internal Family Systems Therapy[SM] is one of the fastest-growing approaches to psychotherapy. It has developed over the past forty years into a way of understanding and treating human problems that is empowering, effective, and nonpathologizing. Internal Family Systems[SM] (IFS) involves helping people heal by listening inside themselves in a new way to different "parts"—feelings or thoughts—and, in the process, unburdening themselves of extreme beliefs, emotions, sensations, and urges that constrain their lives. As they unburden, people have more access to Self, our most precious human resource, and are better able to lead their lives from that centered, confident, compassionate place.

Contents

ACKNOWLEDGMENTS xiii

INTRODUCTION 1

The Three Projects 4

Romantic Rescue: Debbie's Story 5

Becoming the Primary Caretaker of Your Parts 7

The Self 8

Self-to-Self Interaction 9

Speaking for Parts 9

CHAPTER ONE: CULTURAL CONSTRAINTS TO INTIMACY 11

Isolation 11

Cultural Pressure for the Romantic Rescue 12

Staying Out of the Dark Sea 13

The Empty Self 15

Another Kind of Happiness 18

The Cruel Joke 19

Gender Socialization 20

Multiplicity Versus the Myth of the Monolithic Personality 27

CHAPTER TWO: THE DEVELOPMENT
AND POWER OF EXILES 33

The Magical Kitchen Metaphor 33

Well-Fed Parts 36

How Exiles Develop 37

Three Ways Parts Are Exiled 39

We Bury Our Joy 43

The Power of Exiles   43

Finding and Healing Exiles   47

Extreme Beliefs about Relationships   48

Attachment Theory and Exiles   58

Trailheads and Tor-mentors   64

Summary   65

Solution   66

**CHAPTER THREE: COURAGEOUS LOVE
AND DOOMED RELATIONSHIPS**   69

The Neo-Exiles: Parts Exiled by the Relationship   69

The Neo-Exiling Power of Abandonment Anxiety   71

Courageous Love   76

Doomed Relationships   82

The Pros, the Antis, and the Unaffected   87

Noticing Protectors   89

Summary   91

**CHAPTER FOUR: AN EXAMPLE OF GROWING
TOWARD SELF-LEADERSHIP**   95

The Kevin Brady Story   95

The Effects of Trauma   96

Kevin's Protectors   97

Cracked Fortress   98

Protector Fears   100

Going Inside   101

The Suicidal Part   102

Helping Exiles Heal   104

Helen's Work   108

The Couples Sessions   109

Being the "I" in the Storm   111

Speaking For Rather Than From   112

Self-Leadership as a Way of Interacting   114

Reparations   117

Remaining the "I" in the Storm   118

When You Are Your Own Primary Caretaker   119

Anticipating Trouble   121

Partner as Tor-mentor   122

Virtuous Cycles   125

CHAPTER FIVE: GETTING PRACTICAL:
HOW TO BRING IN COURAGEOUS LOVE   129

Following the Relationship Trailhead   130

When a Part Feels Exiled by the Relationship   131

When a Part Is Protecting Hurt or Exiled Parts   133

When a Part Is Polarized with Another Part   134

Revealing Your Parts   135

Self-to-Self Discussions   137

CHAPTER SIX: THE WHOLE PICTURE   151

Conflict   151

Intimacy   155

Good Luck   160

RESOURCES   161

NOTES   163

BIBLIOGRAPHY   167

ABOUT THE AUTHOR   169

Acknowledgments

The words in this book are well earned. I have had relationships with many people that could be considered intimate, and I have learned from all of them. Some of my best teachers have been the clients who have allowed me to experiment with their internal and external families and who have challenged my parts. I'm grateful to them all.

My first wife Nancy taught me a great deal about intimate partnerships and suffered while I was learning. My second wife, Jeanne, while having benefited from that learning, has also helped me to find and heal many more parts—making me realize that this intimacy thing is a life-long process, and I'm so grateful to her for putting up with me.

A lot of the ideas in this book were the product of discussions with IFS senior trainers as we explored how to bring IFS to couples. There were many such contributors, but in particular I want to thank Toni Herbine-Blank, who has an amazing intuition for these issues, and Susan McConnell, who is wise about all kinds of things.

Finally, for much of my career, I have mostly worked with heterosexual, cisgendered couples. That has changed in recent years, although the examples in this book reflect my observations from the majority of my clinical time. I do feel that many of the insights and practices are generally valid regardless of gender identity or sexual orientation, and I also acknowledge that those reading this book who are not heterosexual and/or cisgendered may feel that this book does not adequately give voice to the dynamics and often highly challenging cultural constraints of their intimate relationships.

Introduction

The time will come when, with elation,

you will greet yourself arriving

at your own door, in your own mirror, and each will
smile at the other's welcome and say, sit here. Eat.

You will love again the stranger who was your self.

Give wine. Give bread. Give back your heart
to itself, to the stranger who has loved you
all your life, whom you have ignored

for another . . .

DEREK WALCOTT, *COLLECTED POEMS, 1948–1984*

It's my first session with Kurt and Marissa. Marissa breaks the early tension by stating that they are desperate and I may be their last hope. They have been miserable for four years and have gone through three other marital therapists as well as several weekend retreats for couples. Religiously they practice the communication skills they have been taught and sometimes find them helpful in the moment, but the structure falls apart once either of them touches a sore spot in the other. In therapy they have even found livable compromises to several chronic issues, but their overall dissatisfaction with each other hasn't really changed.

1

Kurt concurs, adding that he feels helpless and despairing. He'd had many relationships but waited to marry until he felt totally sure that he'd found the right partner. He says, "We were so in love, have so much in common, and are both intelligent. Why isn't this working? I've always succeeded in my life. When I find something I want and work hard to get it, I succeed. When I face a problem head-on, I can solve it. This marriage thing is my one big failure."

There are many couples like Kurt and Marissa. Earnestly battling the demons that our culture and its relationship experts implicate, such as poor communication and lack of empathy, they feel bloodied and beaten by their inability to make it work. They alternate between blaming each other and themselves for not being able to bring harmony into their homes and satisfaction to one of the most important relationships in their lives.

What if the premise itself is to blame? What if there were no way that Kurt and Marissa could succeed, no matter how perfect their communication or how much they compromised and empathized? Couples are told that if they could just accommodate each other enough, they would be happy. Each partner is asked what they need from the other, and therapy is designed to find ways that each can change to meet the other's needs. What if there is an essential flaw in this accommodation premise that sets up couples to fail?

I believe that there is. Conditions exist within each partner and in the context of their lives that, if left unchanged, will preclude finding the intimate, mutually supportive, and respectful connection they crave. This book will describe those conditions and offer a clear path to changing them. It will help couples replace the controlling, dependent, possessive, or distant relating they have come to expect and dread with something I call *courageous love*.

When each partner has courageous love for the other, many of the chronic struggles most couples face melt away because each partner is released from being primarily responsible for making the other feel good. Instead, each knows how to care for their own vulnerability, so neither has to force the other into a preconceived mold or control the other's journey.

Courageous love involves accepting all parts of the other because there is no longer a need to keep the other in the confining roles of parent/redeemer/

ego booster/protector. The other senses that acceptance and freedom, which feel wonderful and unusual to them. They come to trust that they don't have to protect themselves from you and can keep their heart open.

Thus this ability to care for yourself emotionally permits the intimacy you seek because you have the courage to allow your partner to come close or get distant without overreacting. With less fear of losing or being hurt by your partner, you can embrace them fully and delight in their love for you.

Is this a far cry from your experience of relationship? Are you thinking, *That sounds nice, but where am I going to find someone who is evolved enough to treat me that way?* You may not have to look as far as you think. If you and your partner can take what I call a *U-turn* (you-turn) in your focus and begin to relate differently inside yourselves, you will each find that courageous love becomes a spontaneous way of life rather than something you must strive to achieve. You will also find that your partner doesn't have to take care of you because there is so much support you can get from yourself.

In our second session, I proposed to Kurt and Marissa that they take that U-turn, and they reacted the way most couples do initially. Marissa said, "I'm willing to look at my part in this, but what about the way Kurt digs at my self-esteem? It's a rare day when he doesn't find something to criticize." Kurt was equally resistant: "Am I supposed to work on myself, so I just accept Marissa's lack of interest in sex? Do you expect me to be okay with a sexless marriage?"

What I propose in this book is a hard sell in Western culture. We are primarily oriented toward getting from our partners what we need to feel good and don't believe we can get much from ourselves. We want to transform the source of pain in the outside world rather than the source within us. That external focus—and the therapies of accommodation that subscribe to it—will only provide temporary relief at best from the inner and outer storms that gradually erode the fertile topsoil of our relationships. There is another way, and we will explore it in this book. Before we do, however, let's further examine the problems with this accommodation premise.

THE THREE PROJECTS

For reasons that will be discussed at length in the pages to come, your partner cannot succeed in making you feel good in a lasting way. For example, if you have had a hard life filled with rejection and loneliness, their love can only temporarily lift the cloud of worthlessness and self-loathing that will return whenever they are away or in another mood. If you enter the relationship expecting them to be that kind of redeemer, inevitably you will be disappointed at some point.

Our Western culture, and many of the relationship experts in it, have issued us faulty maps and improper tools. We've been told that the love we need is a buried treasure hidden in the heart of a special intimate partner. Once we find that partner, the love we crave should flow elixir-like, filling our empty spaces and healing our pain.

When that love stops flowing, even momentarily, we get scared and go to work on one of three projects. The first two of these are designed to get our partner back into that loving redeemer role. The third project is to give up on that endeavor and find alternatives.

The first, and most common, project involves directly trying to force our partner to change back. Some of us get out the blunt saws, scalpels, or dynamite in an attempt to break through the crust surrounding their heart. We plead, criticize, demand, negotiate, seduce, withhold, and shame—all in an effort to get them to change. Most partners resist our crude attempts to perform open-heart surgery on them. They sense the implicit criticism or manipulation behind these change attempts and become defensive.

The second project is to use many of those same crude tools on ourselves. First we strive to figure out what our partner doesn't like about us and then try to sculpt ourselves into what we think they want, even if that is a far cry from our true nature. We use self-criticism and shame to cut out parts of our personalities or pounds off our bodies, hoping that if we please them, they will love us. Because this self-transformation project isn't authentic, it usually backfires, too.

The final project kicks in once we give up on getting the love we crave from our partner. At that point, we begin to close our heart to them and

(1) search for a different partner, (2) numb or distract from the pain and emptiness enough to stay with the original one, or (3) numb and distract enough to live alone.

All of these are exiling projects. In the first, we try to get our partner to exile the parts of them that threaten us. In the second, we work to exile the parts of us that we think they don't like. In the third, we exile the parts of us that are attached to them. As I will discuss later, whenever a relationship creates exiles, it will pay a price.

Although couples enter therapy complaining of all kinds of issues, usually it isn't hard to discern some combination of these three projects behind their dysfunctional patterns of interaction. This is because most of us carry inner vaults full of pain, shame, and emptiness; and most of us know how to deal with these emotions other than to numb or distract from them until we finally get the love of that special other person.

ROMANTIC RESCUE: DEBBIE'S STORY

Best-selling author Debbie Ford describes her own struggle with her inner worthlessness in this way. "By the time I was five years old, I was all too familiar with the voice in my head telling me that I wasn't good enough, that I wasn't wanted, and that I didn't belong. Deep inside I believed there was something wrong with me, and I went to great lengths to conceal my flaws."[1] This statement could have been made by any number of my clients or by me. Each of us then must find ways to manage all that inner angst until we find the person whose love, we have been taught, will make it disappear.

When Debbie was a child, her angst-managing strategy was to use charm and good grades to keep a steady stream of approval flowing into her to drown out the negative voice, until that no longer worked. "When I couldn't find someone to validate me or tell me I was okay, I would sneak across the street to the nearby 7-Eleven and buy a package of Sara Lee brownies and a bottle of Coca-Cola. That dose of sugar really seemed to do the trick." When she was twelve, however, Debbie's parents decided to divorce, and the pain and shame of that sudden event ignited all the burning emotions she had been containing and added to her deep-seated fear that she was flawed, damaged, and had been dealt a bad lot in life.[2]

A version of that plaintive question, "Won't that special someone come and love me?" dwells in most of us and drives our treasure hunts and crude attempts at open-heart surgery. In those dark moments we feel so bereft, so despairing, so alone that some kind of romantic rescue seems like the only real solution. Many messages we get from friends, family, and the media reinforce our attachment to that elusive solution.

Debbie continued to use achievement and perfect appearance to keep her head out of the inner morass of self-loathing but found that they weren't enough. "I began trying to quiet the constant internal noise by drowning myself in drugs. I was hypnotized by the continuous internal dialogue, by the story I told myself over and over again about how I would never make it, how I would never have the love, security, and inner peace I so desperately desired."[3]

Predictably, her frantic search for respite led her on a series of treasure hunts. "In my twenties, I added men to my prescription for pain relief. Unfortunately, my relationships with men always seemed to backfire. They began with a high that held the promise of salvation and ended with a low that left me deeper in the hole than when I began."[4]

That last sentence summarizes the experience of most of us. We feel intense elation when we find our designated redeemer who will love us and prove that we aren't worthless after all—who will provide the salvation we've been seeking.

The problem we will explore in this book is that our partner can no more cleanse our sense of unworthiness than can food, drugs, achievement, or perfect appearance. Consequently, they will disappoint those desperate parts of us, leaving us deeper in the hole of hopelessness and despair, at which point we will initiate one of the three projects discussed earlier.

BECOMING THE PRIMARY CARETAKER OF YOUR PARTS

Fortunately, there is a way to unload the pain and shame that drive these patterns. The first step toward that goal is to shift your focus. Like Debbie, most of us scramble to avoid our inner life and keep our attention fixed on external solutions that include finding or changing a designated redeemer. I try to get couples to do a complete U-turn in their focus, moving them toward, rather than away from, the inner worlds in which they fear to tread.

When people listen deeply inside, they encounter a host of different feelings, fantasies, thoughts, impulses, and sensations that make up the background noise of our everyday experience of being in the world. When people remain focused on and ask questions of one of those inner experiences, they find that it is more than merely a transient thought or emotion. Within each of us is a complex family of subpersonalities, which I call *parts*.[5] These parts are the reasons we can simultaneously have so many contradictory and confusing needs. The American poet Walt Whitman got it right in "Song of Myself": "Do I contradict myself? Very well then I contradict myself. (I am large, I contain multitudes)."[6] So do we all contain multitudes. Thus, the Oracle of Delphi's admonition to "know thyself" should really be to "know thyselves."

I call these often-quarreling subpersonalities parts because when I first started doing this kind of work, that is how my clients referred to them. "Part of me wants to stay married and faithful, but another part wants to be free to get laid every night of the week with a different woman," a client might say. Another would report, "I know I'm successful at my job, but there's a part of me that says it's only a matter of time until my wife finds out how stupid and incompetent I really am." The critical voice that harangued Debbie Ford with so much self-loathing is an example of one common type of part called a *protector*, which tried to keep her from taking risks by running down her confidence. The more vulnerable inner childlike part that believed her critic and, as a consequence, felt worthless and empty is an example of a type of part I call an *exile*.

When I first started doing this kind of work, I was amazed to find that if I could establish a safe, accepting atmosphere in our sessions, clients could have inner discussions with their parts. In a powerful state of internal focus, they could dialogue with their parts about what motivated them to react in such irrational or self-defeating ways. As they listened to their parts' stories, what at first seemed irrational suddenly began to make sense as many parts let the clients know that they were stuck at points in the past when the behaviors or beliefs were understandable and even necessary.

You can become your own healer—the special person your vulnerable parts have been waiting for. When that happens, your partner will be released from the redeemer trap and its accompanying projects, and true intimacy will be possible.

In the past, this wasn't necessarily good news. It meant logging countless hours in a therapist's office, with the two of you speculating together about how you were hurt during your childhoods. Through those insights, you expected to feel less vulnerable, but you often didn't make much progress toward that goal. Fortunately, those days are over because it is now possible to quickly discover the source of your pain and shame and to pump it out of the parts of you that carry it. In the process, those parts come to trust and welcome you as their healer. Then they can love being with your partner.

THE SELF

As clients learn to separate from their extreme emotions and thoughts (their parts) in this way, I find that they spontaneously tap into a calm, centered state, which I call their *Self*. I can sense when this happens in a session because it feels as though the very molecules in the atmosphere have shifted radically. My clients' faces and voices change, growing softer and more tranquil, and they become more open and tender, able to explore their parts without anger, defensiveness, or disdain. In accessing this state of Self, clients are tapping into something deeper and more foundational than all these conflicting inner warriors—something that spiritual traditions often call "soul" or "essence." One aspect of this state is what many therapies call "mindfulness." In this state of Self, clients realize that they already know how to take care of their inner exiles on their own and that those parts don't need salvation because they were never bad to begin with. I refer to this state of Self as *Self-leadership*.

SELF-TO-SELF INTERACTION

I found that when I helped each partner access this state of Self, a dramatic shift occurred in their interactions with each other about problems in their relationship. Their dialogues would be completely different from their usual ones, which were so protective and parts dominated. Even when discussing emotion-laden content, partners could hold a respectful and compassionate tone and were able to listen without defending themselves. Creative solutions, which were so elusive in previous attempts, would emerge spontaneously and without intervention from me.

SPEAKING FOR PARTS

It wasn't that the feelings of clients' parts were absent from the exchanges—oftentimes they were talking about very strong emotions. It's that, because they remained a little separated from their parts, they could speak for those powerful feelings rather than being flooded by them and speaking from them. For example, in the past, Michael would have said to Marcia in a charged, judgmental voice, "I hate the way you interrupt me when I'm trying to make a point." When I was able to help him hold Self-leadership, he said, "When you interrupted me, it triggered an angry part of me that thinks you don't care about my feelings." Michael's tone remained compassionate, and he was able to stay curious about what was happening to Marcia that made her interrupt.

This book is designed to help you do two things that will make a remarkable difference in all your relationships, particularly your romantic ones. The first is that you—your Self—will become the primary caretaker of your exiles so that your partner can be their secondary caretaker. When that is the case, your protectors can abandon all their projects, and you can enjoy your partner for who they are, not what you want them to be. Ironically, in turn, your partner will be better able to drop their guard enough to become vulnerable and reciprocate the love that you seek. The second thing you will gain from this book is that, increasingly, you will be able to interact with your partner from your Self, which not only will resolve, or make far less potent, the long-standing issues between you but also foster the sense of intimacy and deep connectedness that is sustaining to both of you.

I don't want to imply that achieving these goals will be easy. Many beliefs and forces in Western culture run counter to them, and we each carry personal baggage that makes it harder. It will take work, some of which may need to be done with a therapist. This book is designed to reorient that work—to help you work smarter instead of harder.

Let's begin by examining some of the cultural factors that make intimate relationships so challenging.

CHAPTER ONE

Cultural Constraints to Intimacy

Sustaining intimacy wouldn't be such a big problem if you had been encouraged by your family or culture to take care of your exiles. Unfortunately, however, few people know about this secret to relationship success. It is likely that your family taught you the opposite in certain situations—to lock away your parts when they felt hurt, needy, ashamed, or otherwise in pain. Then Western culture bombarded you with messages about how great it would be when you finally found your "soul mate."

ISOLATION

That message about the romance, relief, and redemption to be found in intimate relationships may be required to convince us to enter the extraordinary institution that is American marriage. As the cultural anthropologist Margaret Mead said, "The American marriage . . . is one of the most difficult marriage forms that the human race has ever attempted."[1] Couples were once surrounded by communities of relatives and friends, by people who shared their values and helped them out. Today, couples are frequently isolated, mobile units that are expected to survive on their own. Not only is the couple isolated from its community but each partner is often cut off from the other by the outrageous requirements of work or by the excessive demands of raising children far from the help of kin networks. Indeed, children can be one of the biggest obstacles to intimacy that couples face.

Virtually every study of marital satisfaction has shown that it drops precipitously with the birth of the first child and doesn't recover until the last one leaves. Finally, partners are cut off from their Selves by being raised in a society that is so concerned with external appearances that authentic inner desires are ignored and feared. Into this nearly impossible arrangement is poured the expectation that your partner should make you happy and that if they don't, something is very wrong.

CULTURAL PRESSURE FOR THE ROMANTIC RESCUE

These messages about your partner play into your exiles' dreams, keeping the focus of their yearning on an external relationship rather than on you. Thus the Western culture's view of romantic love as the ultimate salvation exacerbates an already difficult arrangement. Many writers have blamed the unrealistic expectations our culture heaps on marriage as a significant reason for its high rate of collapse. I agree with that indictment to the extent that those expectations perpetuate the partner-as-healer/redeemer syndrome.

In this society, we leave our parents and our children leave us; the only person who is supposed to be with us forever is our partner. As long as we remain such a highly mobile, appearance-obsessed, work- and consumption-addicted culture, our isolated couples do need to find a high degree of satisfaction with each other, especially for those with children, to spare the children the pain of divorce or a sense of responsibility for their parents' well-being.

If we had been taught how to heal our own parts, I believe we would be able to meet many of our needs in an intimate relationship because we wouldn't be as needy. Many expectations of intimate relationships are not unrealistic per se. You can get a great deal from your partner if you are willing to share the responsibility of taking care of your parts rather than placing the onus totally on your partner. When your partner is freed from the extreme pressures to both caretake your parts and deal with your rage or pouting when they don't, your partner can be the lover, companion, and co-adventurer that you want. Once you heal your own exiles, you can drop the drawbridge of your castle and allow your partner enough access to you to create an enjoyable relationship. George complains that he never seems to be able to please his wife, Ann, anymore. He works hard all day and spends most weekday evenings watching their son's soccer games or their daughter's field hockey games. Ann, an accountant, says she also works hard and comes home to a second shift of cleaning the house. She resents George's long hours at work and feels that their lives revolve around careers and kids. On weekends they occasionally socialize with another couple, but they have stopped going out together because they have come to fear the awkward silences when they run out of domestic details to discuss.

George and Ann are seeing a therapist who tries to help them communicate differently. The therapist helps them stop blaming each other and instead gets them to speak about their more vulnerable feelings—George's sense of being a failure as a husband and Ann's loneliness and belief that George prefers work to her. The therapist also has them listen carefully to each other without interrupting and demonstrate that they heard each other by repeating back what was said. They are also given assignments to schedule dates together, to share the household chores more equitably, and to find things to praise about each other. These interventions seem to help. They both report that it makes a big difference when their partner really listens and empathizes with their predicament. In addition, George says that it helps to hear something positive from Ann, and she says that seeing George helping more around the house has lifted her chronic resentment.

STAYING OUT OF THE DARK SEA

George and Ann are typical of many middle-class American couples, and the therapy they received is state of the art. It is the kind of therapy I did with couples for years until I came to realize that, in most cases, the improvements didn't last.

Without a constant stream of affirmation from an intimate partner, most of us will experience these feelings to some degree: worthless, empty, like a loser, lonely, rejected, desperate, ugly, boring, insecure, and afraid.

These are unbearable emotions that we will do anything to avoid. What we call happiness is often relief about not being in those states. Too often our partner becomes a life preserver, keeping our head above water in the dark sea of pain, shame, and fear in which we float. No wonder we feel so threatened and jealous if it looks as though our partner might leave us. And when, for one reason or another, they no longer keep us out of that sea or even push us into it, it's no wonder that we begin to dream of finding a better partner and then go looking for one.

This kind of head-above-water happiness is unstable and easily disturbed. Our partner will buckle under the strain of holding us up, and big waves (such as failures at work or criticism from parents) will wash over us no matter how hard our partner works to save us.

Our culture offers many other life preservers—television, social media, shopping, working, smoking, legal and illegal drugs, alcohol, pornography, prostitution, plastic surgery, diets and exercise, fatty and sweet foods—all the common addictions. As the American novelist John Updike said, "America is a vast conspiracy to make you happy."[2] But these life preservers are flimsy—poor substitutes for human connection. Although they don't keep us afloat for long, these addictive distractions can prevent us from jettisoning intimate relationships by numbing the disappointment we feel when the relationships lose their buoyancy. Or they can opiate our pain when we're between periods of intimate contact. We become convinced that happiness is as close as the next new pair of shoes, a weekend getaway, or a new job.

These distractions become part of a vicious cycle that keeps us addicted to the search for head-above-water happiness and away from a more sustaining happiness. The more we pursue them, the more isolated we become from each other—and ourselves—and the more afraid of the waves around us, so the more desperately we pursue them. To shift metaphors briefly, it's as though we're stuck in a hole and the only tools our culture throws us are an assortment of shovels. As the artist Leonard Cohen sings, "You are locked into your suffering, and your pleasures are the seal."[3]

Exercise

Take a few minutes to reflect on the following questions. Write your answers in a journal that you can keep as you read this book.

What feelings and beliefs do you hold inside that you fear—for example, emptiness, unlovability?

In what ways have you expected your partner to make those feelings disappear?

When do you also rely on the distractions our culture offers, and which of those do you use?

Do you have faith that you could heal the parts of yourself that cause you to have those feelings?

THE EMPTY SELF

Many reasons exist why most of us in this country contain a secret dark sea of lonely emptiness and quiet desperation. Later in the book we will discuss the psychological roots of this condition, but it is also important to consider the sociological development of what the historian Philip Cushman calls the "empty self" that arose in this country after World War II. For Cushman, American individualism lost its soul at that point to the huge pressures of industrial capitalism. Whereas before the war our individualism was tempered by a strong ethic of community service, afterward that changed.[4] The American Dream of ever-upward mobility, fueled by memories of the Great Depression and by increasingly pervasive national advertising, infused that war generation with a more selfish individualism. Their baby-boomer children inherited that perspective and, in addition, experienced less of the extended family and community-focused upbringing that their parents enjoyed. Many of us have lost our connection to connection. As described by the Australian-American author Peter Walsh in his bestselling book *It's All Too Much*, "We live in one of the most prosperous nations on earth, and we measure our success by material accumulation . . . But for many, it has become clear, that instead of bringing us happiness and peace of mind, all this stuff is stressing us out and alienating us from our families, our partners, and our dreams."[5]

The result is the empty self "that experiences a significant absence of community, tradition, and shared meaning . . . a self that embodies the absences, loneliness, and disappointments of life as a chronic, undifferentiated emotional hunger."[6] Our empty selves have been conditioned to sate that hunger with material possessions, which has created a powerful economy that gives us the illusion that we are doing well. But our inner lives are not doing well.

It also hasn't helped that political and other changes in recent decades have made it harder for people in this country to survive financially while we have been bombarded with media images of happy, wealthy, consuming people. The consequent striving for money and exhausting workweeks, whether motivated by the need to stay alive financially or to join the wealthy, leave an ever-larger emotional gulf between ourselves and our families and friends. The fear of falling through the widening holes in our social networks into that dark and lonely sea makes us easy prey for the version of happiness found in the ubiquitous advertisements, so we become more materialistic and have to work even harder to support those materialistic habits. The not-unrealistic fear of sudden financial impoverishment also drives the anxiety and work pace of most people in the United States since the social safety nets have been shredded by years of conservative governing.

To all of us drowning in this oftentimes striving, isolated, and anxious American lifestyle, the media throws the biggest life preserver of all. Media of all types will have you convinced that everyone, sooner or later, will find their one, true, happily-ever-after relationship. The person who will heal you, complete you, and keep you afloat is out there. If the person you're with isn't doing that, either they are the wrong person altogether or you need to change them into the right one.

This is an impossible load for intimate relationships to handle. The striving for money and the isolation from a circle of caring people are enough to do in many marriages—not only because both partners are depleted by the pace of life and absence of nurturing contact but also because to work and compete so hard, they each must become dominated by striving parts that don't lend themselves to intimate vulnerability. To deal with the stress of this lifestyle, we reach for the many distractions that our culture offers, which are also obstacles to, and surrogates for, intimacy.

Recently the United States overtook Japan as the developed country with the workforce that puts in the longest hours. We're spending all our time at work, in places like office cubicles, meeting rooms, and factories; behind computer screens; and on the road to and from our place of work, often removed from nature and from family, friends, and spiritual connectedness. We eat poorly and are out of shape and sleep-deprived. We're anxious about money and our appearance. Add to all that the burden of keeping each other's heads above polluted water, climate change, and social unrest, and it's no wonder so many marriages go under. Stress, depletion, and isolation make it harder to control our inner demons, consequently increasing the pressure on our one intimate relationship to keep the waves of self-loathing and insecurity at bay. This is an impossible task, but we still expect it to work, and we feel like abject failures when it doesn't.

Exercise

How often does your lifestyle allow time and space for intimate exchanges with your partner? What might be getting in the way?

How connected are you and your partner to a network of nurturing relationships?

How much does fear of poverty or competition with others drive your lifestyle?

ANOTHER KIND OF HAPPINESS

Another kind of happiness exists that you can feel steadily whether you are in a relationship or not. It comes from the sense of connectedness that happens when all your parts love one another and trust and feel accepted by your Self. When you have that kind of love swirling around inside you, it spills out to people around you, and those people become part of your circle of love and support. You don't need intimate others to keep you out of the inner dark sea because that sea has been drained of its pain, shame, and fear. In your inner world, your parts are on dry, solid land and are well housed and nourished. They trust you to be their primary caretaker, which allows your partner the freedom and delight that come with being their secondary caretaker.

When you don't fear drowning because there's no longer a dark body of water threatening to swallow you up, and when your inner world is one of abiding love, you don't grasp for the life preservers our culture constantly throws at you. Your material needs are simple, and you value relaxed human connection over nonhuman escape. You have time and energy to nurture an intimate network that extends well beyond your partner, so they aren't the only target of your parts' desires. As the author John F. Schumaker writes regarding his experience during his travels in Tanznia, far away from his home in the US, "For the next hour, I found myself at a little village where I saw more happiness and life enjoyment than I had even before witnessed."[7]

This is also evidenced by the *World Happiness Report*, which over the last years has demonstrated that social support, generosity to one another, and honesty in government are crucial for well-being.[8]

My experience with couples is that living within the American culture where we are often isolated and depleted, it is extremely difficult for even the most psychologically healthy couples to create truly intimate and nourishing relationships. Those of us who carry additional baggage from our personal histories and gender socialization have even higher mountains to climb. Nonetheless try we do, over and over, often without regard to the very challenging nature of the task and filled with self-blame each time we fail.

THE CRUEL JOKE

So we've all been set up—victims of a cruel joke. First we are loaded with emotional burdens by our family and peers and then taught to exile the parts carrying them. Then we are told to go out into the world and find that special person who can make us finally like ourselves. Together we and our partner enter the striving, frenetic-whirlpool American lifestyle that precludes time together, isolates us from community, depletes and stresses us out, and offers innumerable addictive distractions that further isolate us. When we can't make this impossible situation work, we feel like total failures—as though something is wrong with us. We don't realize that we never had a prayer.

Most self-help books and couples therapy approaches collude with this cruel joke. They try to help you fix something that isn't fixable, which makes you feel more like a failure when it doesn't work. Shifting the deck chairs around won't avoid disaster when you're on the *Titanic*. Instead, your relation-ship needs to make a U-turn.

Using structured communication packages, your therapist may convince you both to drop your defenses and open to each other once again. This approach identifies the problem as you and your partner not meeting each other's needs well enough, and it aims to help you negotiate better ways of taking care of each other. Such therapists don't understand that as long as you each contain desperate, orphaned exiles looking to the other for redemption and are caught up in the American whirlwind, that enterprise is futile. Both of you are too depleted, vulnerable, and needy, and too focused on the other for any improvements to last.

After taking a brief history, I frequently tell couples not to feel bad about their failures. Given the baggage with which they entered the relationship and their frantic lifestyle, they never had a chance to sustain real intimacy. Just learning about the cruel joke of which they have been victims often helps couples begin to reverse the vicious cycles it has caused.

The good news is that as you each become more Self-led and experience more inner and outer intimacy, you have less need for material distractions and become more interested in creating community—connecting with the Selves of others around you. During our therapy together, many couples spontaneously find creative ways to downshift their lives and increase their time with each other and with friends and family.

> ## Exercise
>
> In what ways do you feel like a failure in your relationship?
>
> Which of the constraints discussed so far have had a negative impact on your relationship? In what way?

GENDER SOCIALIZATION

This kind of downshifting can be particularly difficult for men, which brings up another cultural influence that cannot be ignored: gender socialization. This is a huge and controversial topic to which I can't do justice in this space. Nor can I discuss it without making gross generalizations that won't apply to many readers. Yet from years of journeying inside with men and women to the source of their protectiveness and pain, several patterns are worth mentioning. In general, boys are taught to value and lead with certain parts of them and to exile others. Girls are socialized to do the same, but with different sets of parts. These differences can create problems in and of themselves, and they challenge the common assumption that women are better equipped to be intimate than men.

A traditional, patriarchal form of child-rearing, dominant in our culture for many decades, was clear in its effects on the inner lives of boys and girls. In that pattern, boys were nurtured by their caretaker (usually their mother) until a certain young age—perhaps four or five—when, out of fear of their being sissified, they were wrenched away and often brutally shamed by their father or by peers for expressions of weakness or any emotions other than aggressiveness and anger—anything considered feminine.

This pattern left many of the men I've treated with extremely needy and fearful exiles that were so thoroughly locked away that most of the time the men had no access to those vulnerable feelings. The term *alexithymia* has been used to describe such men because they are so cut off from those emotions that they don't have words to describe them. Terrence Real, the author of a valuable book on the wounding of men titled *I Don't Want to Talk About It*, describes his life in a way that applies to my own experience and that of many of the men I work with.

> There is a blackness that has lain inside the center of my being. When I have closed my eyes, it has been there. When I have been left alone for more than a few hours, I have returned to it. This jagged, empty, frightening feeling has been a part of my internal atmosphere for as long as I can remember. It has been my baseline, my steady state—the me I spent a good many years running from. I have come to understand that dark, piercing unease at my center as my experience of emotional abandonment and fear of growing up in a dangerous household. It's a little boy's loneliness, which I brought with me out into the world for the next thirty years.[9]

To keep their dark fear and loneliness at bay, men become dominated by rational, aggressive, competitive, never-let-'em-see-you-sweat protectors that can serve them well in professional contexts and are determined to never again allow them to be hurt or humiliated. Men are also taught to bolster their fragile self-esteem by objectifying and pursuing trophy women.

Before the 1960s, when marriages were expected to be more traditional, many men could get through relationships without major challenges to this rigid and limiting inner structure. They weren't interested in being open and emotionally close to their wives, and their wives had been taught not to count on that kind of intimacy from men.

Instead, traditionally raised girls were supposed to be caretakers. They weren't as abruptly abandoned as men by their early source of nurturance nor shamed for being soft, so they remained more connected to their vulnerability and to relationships with their children and female friends. On the other hand, the focus on caretaking others left them little ability to nurture their own vulnerable parts. Whereas men tried to abandon those exiles, women learned to find comfort for them in relationships.

The parts of girls, however, that were bright and assertive, lively and competent, were exiled, and girls became dominated by self-critical protectors that kept them obsessed with the needs of others and with appearing attractive to men. Because of being raised in families where men were more highly valued, these girls also had exiles that felt worthless and focused on the approval of a father who was increasingly threatened by them and who distanced from them as they developed physically.

Since the 1960s, the traditional ways of being men and women have been rightly challenged, creating confusing contradictions for both genders. Now men are still expected to be strong and high-achieving in the outside world, but within their relationship they should be emotionally intelligent—in touch with and open about their feelings and nurturing of their partner's feelings. The protectors they were raised to count on—rational, impatient, action-oriented problem-solvers and entitled, macho objectifiers—are no longer welcome at home.

In this way, men are expected to perform a total reversal of their entrenched inner systems. Suddenly they are supposed to access the very same vulnerable, sensitive, and caring parts that they spent their lives trying to keep locked up. Simultaneously they are expected to exile some of their most trusted protectors. To further confuse things, they need to remain close to the striving, competitive protectors that help them succeed and make lots of money but not bring those parts into the relationship.

It's no wonder that many of the men I treat have shut down. They feel humiliated by their failures in the emotional intelligence department, and humiliation is something they swore early on would never happen to them again (which is why they don't ask for directions). "I feel like I can never satisfy her" is a common male utterance in my office. Since in their relationships they can't rely on aggressiveness or rationality anymore, many men just give up and hide behind stony walls of indifference and passivity, which only further enrages their partners. These men's protectors opt for the third project of becoming resigned to a life of non-intimacy and to finding distractions.

Women, on the other hand, faced their own quandaries as gender expectations shifted. In the post-1960s world, they were expected to shed their subservient and self-sacrificing selves and find their power—the assertive and ambitious parts they had exiled earlier. Within their marriages, this often meant letting their husbands know of their needs for emotional connection and nourishment, and expecting more equity in decision-making and greater access to resources.

The problem is that, similar to men, women were trying to achieve a reversal of entrenched inner systems without knowing how. Consciously or not, their caretaker parts still had a powerful influence, which led them to do more than their share at home (in full collusion with their husbands' entitled parts) while also working outside the home. Those imbalances become combustible when mixed with the chronic disappointment in their husbands' emotional limitations. The inner battles between women's caretakers and their assertive parts often built over time until, seemingly out of the blue, their assertive protectors would explode with an intensity that left their husbands stunned.

The work of the marriage researcher John Gottman is relevant here.[10] Gottman has done his homework, studying over seven hundred couples of all kinds in a laboratory setting and following them over time. Despite differences in how he and I interpret his findings, I will frequently refer to his work in this book because it represents the best data we have on the way couples operate.

He found that men and women are very different in how they handle conflict. For example, in terms of blood pressure and heart-rate changes, men react much more strongly than women when they begin to get into marital conflict, and they stay activated much longer. They may seem rational and calm on the outside, but inside they are having intense emotional reactions to their wives' criticisms.

Men are also more likely to keep angry, vengeful thoughts running through their heads even after the fight is over. Gottman writes, "If you could read their minds, you might hear phrases like, 'I don't have to take this crap,' or 'It's all her fault,' or 'I'll get her back for this.'"[11]

In addition, he found that as the tension builds in couples' fights, men are much more likely than women to shut down emotionally and become what he calls "stonewallers"—people who turn away from and completely ignore their partners in the face of criticism. Indeed, the men were the stonewallers 85 percent of the time during conflict in the relationship.

Women are more likely to bring up issues that lead to arguments and to be critical of their husbands. When he then begins to stonewall, she feels unheard and escalates the argument, leading to a common vicious cycle in which he shuts down more, and she gets increasingly angry as she tries to blast through the stone wall.

Let's review Gottman's findings on gender differences in light of the earlier discussion of men's and women's parts. Given that men have highly vulnerable exiles that they try to keep locked up at all costs, it makes sense that criticism from their wives would trigger the shame those exiles carry, which would account for men's extreme physiological reactions. In addition, men would experience the activation of all their protectors, including defensiveness and even anger or rage. On the playground, boys learned to view criticism as a challenge to their masculinity and to lash out in response. As we've discussed, men's angry parts aren't welcome in many marriages. Also, many men fear what they might do to their partner if they let rage take over. So they are left with few alternatives. They are loathe to expose and don't have words to describe the intense vulnerability they feel, and their customary protectors are taboo. Shutting down externally seems like the safest choice while, as Gottman found, internally their stifled angry protectors continue to roil beneath the surface and keep them stirred up.

Far more than men, women are socialized to take care of their exiles through relationships. Therefore, when their exiles are upset, women want to change things in their marriages so that their distressed exiles get from their husbands the love and comfort those parts need to feel secure. Hence women are more often the initiators of change-oriented discussions and are frustrated and critical when those discussions are aborted by their husbands' stonewalling. In addition, because of the collusion between women's caretaker parts and men's entitled ones, real imbalances often exist in the lifestyles of each spouse—the wife has more responsibility and fewer resources—that fuel her rage and his reluctance to talk.

In terms of the three projects, mentioned earlier, that protective parts take on in relationships once exiles have been hurt, it seems that women are more likely to keep plugging away with the first two, while men more quickly retreat to the third. That is, because women want a relational solution to their pain, their inner critics take aim at their husband and, when that doesn't work, at themselves, in an effort to open his heart. Men, partly in response to what feels like intolerable criticism, will give up sooner on the intimacy-generating projects and will focus instead on distractions that make them feel good, such as work, sports, and drinking alcohol.

Many men's exiles are so well insulated from them that it often seems that they don't need intimacy. The fallacy of that myth is exposed when, for example, their partner decides they have finally had enough and threatens seriously to abandon them. At that point, many men's protective fortresses crack open and their raw, needy exiles break through and take over. I've seen husbands who a day earlier had seemed aloof, totally in control and independent, transform into desperate, pleading little boys when facing abandonment from their wives. Despite being extremely isolated inside, these childlike parts of the husbands were addicted to the little affection from their wives that was allowed to trickle down to these exiles through the walls of protection. The exiles knew that this trickle was all that kept them from a return to utter love-starvation and worthlessness. This phenomenon also explains why some men who seem so detached from their spouses are simultaneously so possessive and jealous, to the point of stalking and threatening them when they try to leave.

I'll end this section on gender differences by reiterating a couple of points. The first challenges a prevalent belief in our culture and among couples therapists—the assumption that because women are closer to their feelings and are more relational than men, they are better equipped for intimacy. In contrast, I believe that because women's focus is so much on caretaking others and on getting their exiles cared for by a relationship, they are no better at nurturing their own parts than are men.

The second point is that these gender patterns are not exclusively due to biological differences in vulnerability or emotionality. While biological differences exist and should not be minimized, both genders have been socialized to create exiles. Many of the incompatibilities between men and women come from differences in how they were trained to relate to those needy parts inside and outside. When it comes to achieving intimacy, both men and women are expected to reverse various rigid internal systems without an instruction manual. Fortunately, once they learn how to care for their own exiles and lead from their Selves, many of the polarizations resulting from their confusing socializations dissolve.

Exercise

Where do you see highly rational, competitive, striving parts showing up in your life and in your relationships?

When do you avoid bringing up issues, or when do you shut down conversations around issues? How do you feel about conflict?

Do you have expectations that your partner will be nurturing and soft? How high are these expectations?

How hard are your caretaking parts working? How much access do you have to your assertiveness—to your ability to ask directly for what you need? How hard is it to feel okay when distance exists in your relationship?

Do you have expectations that your partner
will be strong and take care of you?
How high are these expectations?

The LGBTQIA+ community is also subjected to the same problematic socialization process and, in addition, carries burdens of shame about their sexuality and about being different. In more traditional families, not only are they trained to exile the same parts as straight boys and girls but also they are forced to exile their sexual desires. The shame can produce parts full of self-hate, as well as other parts carrying rage at how they have been treated. These extra burdens can make relationships even more challenging than for those in the hetero world.

I have worked with many LGBTQIA+ clients in individual therapy but not many in couples therapy. The examples in this book are drawn from my clinical experience and, consequently, are of heterosexual couples. I believe, however, that much of the theory and all of the techniques can be applied to same-sex couples as well.

MULTIPLICITY VERSUS THE MYTH OF THE MONOLITHIC PERSONALITY

One other cultural influence has a pervasive and toxic effect on intimate relationships. I call it the *myth of the monolithic personality*—the belief that we have but one mind from which emanate various thoughts and feelings. It is no exaggeration to say that the myth of the monolithic personality is one of the greatest causes of distance in and dissolution of intimate relationships and that awareness of our natural multiplicity is the greatest antidote. Why is it much easier to stay happily partnered with someone with many parts to their personalities than a person you think has just one? For one thing, when your partner says they no longer love you, things get pretty bleak if you think that's their unitary personality speaking. For another, it is much easier not to write off your partner when you know you have an inner family with lots of different perspectives and desires than when you take as gospel all the intense feelings about your partner that come up inside you during the dance of intimacy.

While the notion of yourself as containing autonomous multitudes may be disconcerting, the multiplicity perspective offers a great deal of good news for couples. First, during the inevitable dark periods in the relationship when you find your love for them leaking out of your heart like air out of a balloon, and your mind is reminding you of all their faults and wishing they would move out or die so you could finally be free, it is terrifying to believe that those are your most authentic feelings, thoughts, and desires. If you don't love them anymore, why are you still with them?

How can you be so selfish as to want them to die? What's wrong with you that you can't make relationships work? These kinds of panicked and caustic inner questions make sense if you believe that you are a unitary personality. If your love has disappeared and your partner now disgusts you, it makes sense that you should move on. If you believe that your one mind wishes they were dead, it follows that you must be a terrible person to harbor such a desire.

If, on the other hand, you recognize that your sudden absence of love is caused by the activation of protective parts of you that have blocked your love in the way that the moon obscures the sun during an eclipse, you can trust that there is no need to panic or do something rash. Instead, you use that numbing experience to signal the need to listen inside to discover why you've become so protective and what needs to change, both internally and externally, to help your protectors trust that it is safe to open your heart again.

Similarly, you will react very differently to daydreams about their death if you realize that you have young, childlike parts that, when frustrated, have a variety of immature and selfish fantasies. Rather than loathing yourself and trying to suppress those thoughts, you can treat yourself with the kind of amused patience and understanding that a parent might bring to their angry two-year-old who just said, "I hate Daddy and I wish he would die!"

Knowledge of our multiplicity also helps when your partner says hurtful things or acts in extreme ways. When, in the middle of a fight, they say that they can't stand you and wish they never married you, those words are much less devastating if you trust that they came from a young, tantrumming part of them than if you believe that they are finally revealing their true feelings. When, after a failure at work, they seem insecure and scared, it is much better for your relationship that you think to yourself, *That failure just triggered their scared parts*, rather than *I had no idea they were such a coward*.

The ability to hold the multiplicity perspective about yourself and your partner is enhanced by the simple (but often difficult) act of speaking for, rather than from, your parts. If, when you get angry, you say, "A part of me hates you right now," your partner gets an entirely different message than if you say, "I hate you right now." This is not just because the former words remind your partner that it is just a part, not all of you. It is also because in speaking for a part, you have to separate from it to some degree, so what you say doesn't carry the same level of charge or contempt as when the part totally hijacks you and you speak from it. Later in this book, we will explore in depth this practice of speaking for, rather than from, your parts. For now, the point is that anything that reminds you and your partner that you both have a multiplicity of parts, and that you both have a Self in there somewhere, helps hold connection even during the perfect storms in your relationship.

Also, when you separate from a part, more of your Self emerges spontaneously. When some degree of Self is present in your communication to your partner, they will sense a tone of respect and caring, even in messages whose content holds a challenge or complaint. While it is a very rare person who can hold total Self-leadership in the middle of a hot conflict with an intimate partner, it is possible for you to avoid becoming so thoroughly blended with your parts that you lose all perspective. I find that if couples can maintain even a small degree of Self-to-Self connection while they fight, the damage from the storm is minimal and the repair comes quickly.

Even during the worst storms, when both of you are totally flooded by extreme protectors, the knowledge that this isn't a permanent condition—that the clouds will part and the sun will shine again; that the protectors on both sides will relax and your two Selves will emerge eventually—is very comforting and can keep panic from setting in. Once your Selves reemerge, repair and reconnection are possible. People can tolerate a great deal of scary turbulence if they trust that smooth skies are just ahead. As we will discuss later, it's only when protectors come to permanently dominate interactions that relationships are doomed.

Not only does the multiplicity perspective help you through the inevitable storms of couplehood but it can also deepen the intimacy you came together to achieve. One aspect of intimacy is the ability to be highly vulnerable with your partner and, while in that state, to receive love and acceptance from them. It is scary to reveal to anyone, but especially to your intimate other, aspects of your character that you view as weak, unsavory, or shameful. The fear is that once you expose those parts of you, you will be forever seen by that other as having those character flaws. If you both understand that those are just small parts of you—parts that carry burdens of worthlessness, insecurity, distorted sexual impulses, and so on; parts that simply need empathy and acceptance to heal—it's easier for you to reveal them and for your partner to respond lovingly.

There is something magical about trusting that all of you is welcomed in a relationship. It's as if you are a single parent who feels ashamed of some of your children's behavior and thinks they reflect badly on you. Then you find someone who not only accepts them but who also can see past their apparent deficits to their essential goodness and lovability. You feel an incredible connection to that person, based not only on relief at no longer having to hide your children from the world but also on seeing how they make the children shine and how attached they are to that person.

When this process of vulnerability and acceptance is mutual, couples form such a secure connection that their protectors relax, and their young parts know it's safe to pop out at any time. You may know a couple whose relationship seems full of lively spontaneity and creative playfulness. They literally bring out the best in each other because they each know that all their parts are welcome to step into the warm, safe space between them. Their interactions have the feel of an improv ensemble, with a wide variety of characters jumping excitedly onto the stage and playing off each other.

Actually, you may have had trouble thinking of a couple you know like that. Unfortunately, such vibrant relationships are rare because without the multiplicity perspective and the knowledge of how to hold Self-leadership, it is very difficult not to overreact to the extremes of some of your partner's parts. You resent their sloppiness because you think they want you to do all the housework. They blow up at you for nagging about cleanliness, assuming that you are a control freak. Your need to stay out of debt makes them think that you don't trust their judgment about money. Their cavalier attitude about spending leaves you with the impression that they don't care how hard you have to work to earn money. When your partner chronically acts in ways that bother you, you tend to: (1) assume that behavior represents a core personality trait that you're stuck with and (2) attribute a selfish or pathological motive to the behavior. Because of these monolithic attributions, you will be critical or contemptuous of your partner, and they will respond in kind.

The result of processes like these is that each partner retreats behind walls of indifference or caution. The playful and loving parts that initially brought them together are bruised and now seem too vulnerable to reveal. The alert system between them shifts from green to amber and, sometimes, even to red. Their interactions become stilted and predictable because only a few members of their respective inner parts do the interacting, and those members don't trust one another. Many parts of each partner feel most unwelcome. Those parts will leave you with an underlying sense of emptiness and dissatisfaction, and, at some point, these parts will give up hope and begin to sabotage.

The rest of this book is designed to help you avoid becoming an amber or red couple or, if you are already on high alert, help you get back to green. If you ever had a vibrant energy between you, you can get it back. Having a general knowledge about parts and Self can help a great deal, and in the coming pages I will embellish the framework we have developed so far and add exercises and techniques that can lighten the load your relationship carries.

Exercise

Following the experience of extreme beliefs and emotions in your relationship, what feelings come up for you? Shame? Anger? Resentfulness? How do these extreme beliefs and emotions make themselves known to you?

Do you take the extreme things your partner says or does as representative of a core personality trait? If so, how does that affect the way you feel about the relationship?

What would change in your relationship if you trusted that these extreme beliefs and emotions came from small, burdened parts of you and your partner?

CHAPTER TWO

The Development and Power of Exiles

THE MAGICAL KITCHEN METAPHOR

Before we explore the development and power of exiles, I want to offer a way into understanding this material. The spiritual teacher and author Don Miguel Ruiz uses the metaphor of the magical kitchen to describe intimate relationships.[1] I will embellish his metaphor to illustrate what happens with our parts.

Imagine that you inherited from your parents a magical kitchen in your home from which you can obtain any kind and quantity of food. Because your parents fed you unconditionally, you learned to do the same with your many children. They are happy because they love your food. Your food is so nourishing and satisfying that they never overeat or crave candy or other kinds of junk food. You never use food to punish or motivate them; consequently, they trust that they are worthy of being well fed just because they are your children. They don't fight because each one knows there is plenty of food for everyone. You also give freely to friends, neighbors, and those in need of food, just for the pleasure of sharing. You know that you don't need to hoard because your food supply never runs out.

Then one day a man knocks on your door and offers your children a steady supply of pizza and candy if they will take care of him emotionally. Because you and your kids are so full and you can see that he doesn't take good care of his own kids, your response is, "No, thank you—we have plenty of food of our own."

On another day, a different man knocks. He is like you in that he has many children whom he feeds generously and who are happy and satisfied. He is attracted to the cuisine of your magical kitchen, but he doesn't need it because he likes to cook and has plenty of food of his own. His children love playing with yours and would like to live in your house, but because they know that he will care for them no matter what happens with you, they trust him to decide where to live.

You invite him to share your home, and you love how much the two of you enjoy each other's cooking. Both sets of children relish the mixed cuisine that now comes from your kitchen.

Now imagine that you live in a different household. You are very poor and have little food for your children. Because they are starving, the youngest and weakest of your kids cry all the time and beg you to find someone to feed them. Their desperation is extremely frustrating, and you ground them in their room frequently so that they aren't always in your hair and you're not always reminded of their suffering. That's the way your parents taught you to handle problem children.

As hard as you try to ignore the sobs of those young ones, however, you can still hear them through the floorboards. The urgency of their need is like a constant gnawing in the back of your mind. Some of your older children lose trust in your ability to take care of the family. They take on adultlike responsibilities, prodding you to work harder, trying to contain or calm the ones in the basement, and searching for food. Because these older ones aren't equipped to handle this level of responsibility, they become rigid and controlling. They are constantly critical of your work habits and performance, and they expend enormous amounts of energy trying to keep the bedroom basement children at bay.

As the guy with the pizza and candy heads toward your door, the basement children smell the food before he arrives. They are overflowing with joy at the prospect of being fed and possibly released from their exile. They idolize the Candy Man and are willing to do anything to please him. You and the older kids are hungry, exhausted, and impressed by how happy the Candy Man makes the basement children feel. The possibility is very appealing of no longer having to deal with them and instead letting them attach to someone else.

Consequently, despite some misgivings about the guy's demands and the poor quality of his food, you and the older children agree to satisfy his emotional needs in return for steady meals. He turns out to be abusive at times, but your younger kids fear starving and being returned to the basement. Also, while he is increasingly stingy with the pizza and candy, the younger kids are addicted to it. Every time you bring up the topic of throwing him out, they override you.

Now imagine that the food in this story is really love, and the children are the different parts of you. If you identify with the first parent, who has the magical kitchen, you don't need to read the rest of this book. That's because when you love and accept your parts unconditionally—simply because they are in you—they won't be attracted by the false promises of certain other people. And when you find the right partner, your parts won't be so dependent, demanding, protective, or easily hurt that they create constant dramas or make you tolerate abuse. Instead, they each will love your partner in their different ways, enriching your experience of intimacy, secure in the knowledge that if they are hurt by the partner, you are there for them and will deal with it.

If you are like many people, however, you learned from parents, peers, and other influences to exile certain parts of you. Therefore, the basement of your psyche is filled with love-starved, vulnerable inner children. Because they get so little from you, they will be obsessed with finding someone they imagine can rescue them and, out of their desperation, will blind you to that person's faults. So they are likely to make you pick the wrong person and then, because they are so needy and vulnerable, will either make you stay with that person too long, overreact to perceived hurts from them, or try to control how close or distant they get to you or to others.

So where can you find the equivalent of a magical kitchen—a boundless fountain of love from which your parts can draw? It's in the last place you would ever think to look: your Self. But your parts have been convinced by messages from others and by the way you've treated them in the past that their only hope for finding the love they crave is in the outside world.

WELL-FED PARTS

This notion is not entirely a myth. Your parts can get a great deal from another person. But that is only possible if they already have a loving relationship with you. In this book, you will learn how to become the primary caretaker of your parts so that your partner can be their secondary caretaker.

Many books on improving relationships contain some version of the truism that you can't really love another person until you love yourself. In most of those books, the idea of loving yourself is held up as an abstract ideal to strive for, or else you are given affirmations to repeat as a way to counter all your negative self-talk. In this book, you will find concrete ways to tap into the magical kitchen of your Self, which will allow you to love even your carping self-critics and your basement children. And you will find that, just as is true of well-fed children in the outside world, your inner characters will transform—they'll become lighter and happier—when you feed rather than starve them. When that's the case, they will enhance rather than encumber your intimate relationships.

Your partner will appreciate this arrangement because they won't feel the weight of your emotional dependence or the sting of your rage when they are unintentionally neglectful. Your parts will look first to you rather than your partner for their sustenance and for comfort when they are hurt. With this arrangement, your parts can stay calm and not panic when your partner distances, not fear being hurt when they get close, and allow your partner to be who they are rather than make them into the image of the person they have been dreaming of. When your partner cries, shows fear, or otherwise acts like one of your vulnerable parts, you can lovingly comfort them because you know how to do that with those parts of you. When your partner is angry, you don't have to get defensive because you don't have a nasty inner critic that is agreeing with and amplifying their criticism of you. When your partner is shy, you don't begin to judge them since you are accepting of the shy part of you. In other words, because you can love all kinds of parts of you, you can love your partner even when they're acting like those parts. It's all connected—how you relate internally directly translates into how you relate externally and vice versa.

Intimacy is often defined as the ability to reveal all aspects of oneself to another and feel accepted. Because you aren't ashamed or afraid of your vulnerable parts, you can expose them to your partner and experience the joy of being fully known and witnessed by another. When your partner is similarly vulnerable, you can be lovingly present with them but not feel as though you have to fix anything. You can have a relationship in which all parts are truly welcome. Even when your partner distances or is angry, your sensitive parts don't panic because they trust that whatever happens with your partner, they still have your love.

When all that is the case, you will be able to bask in the radiance of your partner's love because you won't fear losing it or being engulfed by it. When life hurts or scares your parts, they have two sources of solace: your Self and your partner. When your partner acts like someone from your past—your parents, for example—and this activates unhealed wounds that make you feel horrible, you are able to speak for, rather than from, those wounded parts because they trust you to represent them well.

Consequently, you communicate your hurt with clarity and respect, without the blaming or pouting that commonly typifies such interactions. In turn, your partner is able to act in a compassionate manner, which helps your parts revise their beliefs about intimate relationships and unload the pain they carry from the past. In this way, your partner can help you heal without carrying the heavy load of being your healer.

HOW EXILES DEVELOP

Because our exiles and the parts that protect them have such power over our ability to be close to our partners, we will explore in some detail how exiles develop and why they have such power in our relationships.

Everyone is born with vulnerable parts. Most of us, however, learn early—through interactions with caretakers or through traumatic experiences—that being vulnerable is not safe. As a consequence, we lock those childlike parts away inside and make them the inner exiles of our personalities.

On the other hand, some people are lucky enough to have caretakers who react to their vulnerability with love, patience, tenderness, and nurturance. If that was true for you, you don't have as many exiles. Because your caretakers accepted and embraced you when those sensitive parts of you were present, you learned to relate to those parts in the same way—with acceptance and love.

To give an example, Simon grew up with a learning disorder. His older brother was a good student who was lavishly praised at home and at school for his grades. Out of his hurt and frustration, Simon was often whiny, clingy, and demanding of his mother's attention. Rather than criticize or punish him for acting that way, Simon's parents were able to see the pain that drove his immature behavior. While they set limits at times when his hurt part was expressing itself in that indirect, demanding way, they kept their hearts open, even while being firm. More importantly, they created relationships with him in which he felt safe to tell them about feeling like a failure and a loser. Rather than trying to convince Simon that he was better than his brother in other areas or telling him to think about the positive things in his life, his parents were able to just listen to his pain and show Simon that they loved him no matter how he performed.

Because his parents related to Simon's hurt part with such compassion, patience, and love, whenever Simon felt bad because he couldn't read the way everyone else could, he would comfort that hurt part of himself in the same way—that is, he would listen to the pain and give it love. As a result, that young, vulnerable, childlike part felt securely connected to him, and when it wasn't hurt, it continuously provided Simon with a sense of wonder about the world and a delightful playfulness.

If Simon's parents had instead reacted the way many parents do to such "babyish" behavior—with criticism and impatience—when Simon sensed the hurt, he would have criticized himself and banished his hurt to an inner basement. As an adult, Simon would have wound up cut off from that wonder and playfulness, and would be dominated by critical and impatient parts—his managers. He would have become one of those insensitive and emotionally unavailable men women complain about who are afraid of and removed from all feelings except anger and cynicism.

Since manager-dominated people don't experience much connectedness, his partner would have complained of feeling objectified, as though his only interests were sex and making himself look good.

In addition, he would have a chronic dull ache in the pit of his stomach coming from that exiled part, which would become the background music of his life. His protectors would find ways to anesthetize or distract him from the ache such that if you asked how he was doing, most of the time he'd say "Fine" and would mean it. The exception to fine would occur when something in the outside world—a small slight or failure—touched that open sore. At those times, it would feel as though his gut exploded with flames of pain as he was pulled back into the morass of stored humiliations from his childhood.

Even though Simon wouldn't be consciously aware of it, that chronic ache and the possibility of it exploding would become a major organizing force in his life. He might become a workaholic, striving constantly to distract from the ache, achieve enough to prove he wasn't a failure, and become attractive enough that no one would reject him. If he did fail at something, he might go on a drinking binge to douse the flames of emotion erupting from his gut. And, most relevant to this book, he would expect the mate he found to heal or redeem him—to eliminate that throbbing ache.

THREE WAYS PARTS ARE EXILED

Intimacy problems are driven by a background ache, sense of emptiness, or pool of shame. When, as children, our parts were upset and consequently became extreme in one way or another—selfish, shy, agitated, tantrumming, demanding, hitting, acting out sexually, fearful, and so on—we triggered parts of our parents because they had no patience for those same parts in themselves. So our parents reacted to us with criticism, rage, withdrawal of affection, and harsh punishments. Maybe that wasn't always their reaction, but they did it often enough to make us fear, loathe, and exile those parts of us.

Consequently, when you were hurt, needy, pouty, demanding, tantrumming, or crying, it would trigger your caregiver to react in an extreme way rather than with the warm nurturance or calm limit-setting that your parts needed.

Perhaps your father disdained his own vulnerability as effeminate and consequently shamed you for yours. Or your mother so needed you to care for her that she gave you the message that you couldn't have needs of your own. Suppose, in addition, that as you grew up, your peers humiliated you when you were open and spontaneous, and that when you told your parents or friends of that humiliation, they told you to get over it, to forget about it. Our exiles are often our most sensitive parts because they are the ones most hurt by the rejections, humiliations, traumas, and abandonments of our harsh environment and, while in their state of hurt or need, the parts that most trigger the people around us.

Perhaps, however, it wasn't just when your young parts were upset and extreme that they were punished. Many families have unspoken rules against certain kinds of expressions such that a child's simple natural exuberance, sexuality, or assertiveness is labeled as showing off, selfish, disgusting, and sinful. To survive in such a family, you adopted your family's attitude toward those parts of you and exiled them, too.

From those kinds of experiences, many of us learned to disdain, stifle, and try to eliminate not only our neediness and vulnerability but also our liveliness. We locked away our vitality, passion, sensuality, and courage because those qualities threatened someone we depended on. I have worked with many clients who were told by their family that they were "too much" and who had playfulness and daring shamed out of them.

There are three primary reasons you wound up exiling your most precious aspects.

Your Vulnerability, in Its Natural, Innocent State, Bothered Your Caretakers or Peers

This happened if your caregivers were:

depressed or in conflict with each other such that there was no room for your neediness and, instead, you had to worry about and care for them;

neglectfully preoccupied such that you had to raise yourself and/or your siblings;

using you as a surrogate spouse or living vicariously through your achievements;

convinced that you had to be tough to survive or highly competitive to succeed; or

afraid or disdainful of their own neediness and, consequently, were verbally or physically abusive.

It also happened if your peer group was focused on being cool, tough, or competitive.

Your Natural Vitality Disturbed Your Caretakers or Peers

This happened if one or both of your parents were:

adherents of a rigid religious tradition that viewed various natural expressions as sinful;

afraid to let you grow up and leave them because of being highly dependent on you;

survivors of sexual or physical abuse such that any sexuality or aggression in you was threatening;

violent with each other or sexually acting out such that you became afraid of assertiveness or sexuality;

afraid of their own vitality and, consequently, were verbally or physically abusive when you showed liveliness; or

convinced that in order to attract a partner, you needed to be submissive or nonthreatening.

It also happened if your peer or sibling group was highly aggressive or demeaning such that you retreated from the fray.

Your Vulnerable or Lively Parts Were Hurt, Became Extreme Because of the Hurt, and Then Triggered Other People or Disturbed You

This happened when you were (to give a few examples from my clinical work):

> displaced by the birth of a sibling, so you pouted and tantrummed and then were severely scolded;
>
> secretly sexually molested by a family member, so you began acting out sexually with other children and were harshly punished;
>
> attacked by a bully at school, felt as though you never wanted to leave the house, and locked up the fear so you could return to school; or
>
> shocked by the sudden death of a parent, wanted to collapse with grief and never get out of bed, and locked away the grief so you could function.

When exiling happens for the first two reasons, exiles will feel rejected and unlovable. Because of our culture's beliefs about gender, the first kind of exiling happens more often with boys and the second with girls. The third kind happens to all genders. When exiling happens for the third reason, exiles experience insult added to injury. They carry the memories, sensations, beliefs, and emotions of the hurtful experiences; then they are rejected by others as well as by us.

Exercise

How did your parents or family react to you when you were vulnerable? When you were lively? When you were hurt and, consequently, were extreme?

How did their reactions affect the way you learned to relate to those parts of you?

WE BURY OUR JOY

Our exiles are a buried treasure that, because they are in a state of tremendous pain and need, we experience as toxic waste and remain convinced that if we get near them, we will be contaminated. Everyone around us agrees that we shouldn't go there and instead should just get over it and not look back. This is because no one understands that what is toxic are the emotions and beliefs the exiles carry—their burdens—not the exiled parts themselves. On the contrary, those parts are the vulnerability, sensitivity, playfulness, creativity, and spontaneity that are the heart of intimacy. How can we expect to enjoy our partner when we've buried our joy? When relationships seem bland and tasteless, each partner blames the other without realizing that they both forgot where they hid the spice.

So the exiling of a vulnerable part is akin to first shaming a child and then locking them in a dark dungeon. A young child in that situation feels terrible—rejected and abandoned, scared and needy, unlovable and desperate for redemption. That's exactly how many exiled childlike parts of us feel.

THE POWER OF EXILES

The parts we exile exert far more control over us than an imprisoned child could over the people who locked them up. Unlike the imprisoned child, these exiles, when they are hurt by something that happens in our lives, have the power to pull us into their despair. We become them, suddenly swallowed up by their pain and shame in terrifying ways.

The author Elizabeth Gilbert tells how her exiles began taking over when her boyfriend, David, began rejecting her. She captures well the hell we enter while in this state.

> I came to fear nighttime like it was a torturer's cellar. I would lie there beside David's beautiful, inaccessible sleeping body and I would spin into a panic of loneliness and meticulously detailed suicidal thoughts. Every part of my body pained me. I felt like I was some kind of primitive spring-loaded machine, placed under

far more tension than it had ever been built to sustain, about to blast apart at great danger to anyone standing nearby. I imagined my body parts flying off my torso in order to escape the volcanic core of unhappiness that had become: me. Most mornings David would wake to find me sleeping fitfully on the floor beside his bed, huddled on a pile of bathroom towels, like a dog.[2]

When our exiles hijack us this powerfully, they often trigger surprise and then revulsion in our partners, which is the opposite of what the exiles want and compounds their sense of rejection.

As this happened with David, Elizabeth became increasingly desperate.

I was despondent and dependent, needing more care than an armful of premature infant triplets. His withdrawal only made me more needy and my neediness only advanced his withdrawals, until soon he was retreating under fire of my weeping pleas of "Where are you going? What happened to us?". . . the object of your adoration has now become repulsed by you. He looks at you like you're someone he's never met before, much less someone he once loved with high passion. The irony is, you can hardly blame him. I mean, check yourself out. You're a pathetic mess, unrecognizable even to your own eyes.[3]

In Elizabeth's final sentence lies yet another component of the intractable vicious cycle that begins when exiles hijack. You come to hate the fact that you are acting so weak and clinging, and can see what it's doing to your partner yet you can't stop yourself. Your inner critics frantically try to shame you out of it and try to lock up your exiles again, which only makes your exiles feel worse about themselves and more desperate, so they take over more. It's likely that David, like many men, hated his own needy exiles, so when he saw Elizabeth acting that way, he reacted to her the same way he reacted to his own—with distance and contempt.

The Internal Family Systems (IFS) therapist Mona Barbera offers another example of this process in her valuable book *Bring Yourself to Love*. She describes a time when she had been trying to get her husband, Monk, to go with her to a couples workshop and he refused.

> I started to lose my relaxed . . . feeling and get tense. Suddenly I was twelve years old, sitting at the dinner table, with Mom on my left, Dad on my right, and sister Lana directly across. There was a bowl of creamy, homemade tomato soup in front of me, and I wasn't eating it. Mom asked why, and I said I didn't like it. Her face seemed to work for a second or two, and then she erupted out of her chair, yelling "You are an ungrateful, hurtful, hateful child. I can never please you!" and pounded up the stairs to her room. We all knew from experience that she wouldn't be down for three days, and it didn't matter if we knocked or pleaded or said we were sorry.
>
> As I sat at that table with my sister and father, I kept very still on the outside so I wouldn't upset anyone anymore. On the inside, a shield was forming around my gut feelings so that I wouldn't know what they were, and I wouldn't get hurt from expressing them.
>
> When Monk said, "I don't want to do a couples workshop," he triggered this twelve-year-old part of me. It was as though I were a child, back with my family. All I could hear in my head was, "He doesn't ever care about my needs! It doesn't matter what I want." I didn't know this was only part of me because its reality was consuming me. I couldn't notice the hurt twelve-year-old, and I couldn't be there for her.
>
> I didn't show the hurt to Monk. Instead, angry parts immediately came out to accuse my husband of not caring and not being fair. And, of course, my angry parts stimulated his angry, attacking parts.[4]

As Mona found, these exiles are frozen in time during scenes we want to forget. When triggered, some of us react the way Elizabeth did, becoming overwhelmed and showing our partner our hurt and neediness. Others of us are more like Mona, feeling the exile's excruciating pain inside but never letting our partner see it. Instead, we lead with an explosively angry protector, bewildering our partner with the intensity of our reaction. It's likely that Mona's unprovoked, out-of-the-blue eruption scared a comparable exile in Monk that took him to an equally dark place in his past and fueled his protective retaliation. This is how fights escalate with couples. Their protectors hurt their vulnerable exiles, thrusting them each into the past and engendering ever more extreme protection and hurt.

In addition, when exiles are not triggered and instead exist in us as a chronic background ache, they still powerfully, although unconsciously, influence many aspects of our lives, including our choice of intimate partner, our ability to be patient during the search for that partner, and the degree to which we cling to, try to control, protect ourselves from, are hurt by, and are dissatisfied with that partner. In other words, our exiles and their protectors determine everything about our success and failure with intimacy. Your exiles suffered a double whammy. First they were rejected, shamed, or abandoned by someone you relied on to love you, and then you rejected, shamed, and abandoned them. As a result, they are often desperate to be loved yet also desperately afraid that they will lose any love they get or are convinced they don't deserve any. As I said earlier, in their exiled state, they seem less like buried treasure than toxic waste that will contaminate everything if you let it out. While in that state, these exiles can wreak havoc on your relationships.

So it makes sense for everyone to tell you not to go there. It takes a leap of faith to get close to your exiles. You have to trust that they are more than they seem and that they can transform into valuable qualities. One goal of this book is to convince you that while your exiles are destructive to your relationships, they are only that way because they have been exiled and carry burdens from your past. Once you learn to love and care for them yourself, they will become the very qualities that make relationships sparkle.

FINDING AND HEALING EXILES

Because Mona knew about parts and how to find them inside, later she was able to find and comfort that miserable teenage part and then reconnect with Monk.

> Several hours later, on a dirt road outside a . . . restaurant, I was finally able to recognize the hurt twelve-year-old within me. I met her where she felt trapped and isolated in that dining room. I felt her relax with my presence and my acknowledgment of her world. . . I was doing for her what no one else had done—noticing her pain. I emerged out of my narrow self-focus and saw Monk standing there in the dark, his shoulders tense and his face blank and hard. He was in pain, too!
> . . . I took a deep breath, gave up my angry attitude, and said, "I must have hurt you very much for you to be acting this way."

His shoulders dropped and his face softened into its familiar contours. I felt my own tension go away, and I felt a rich, warm, grounded feeling in my center—our connection.[5]

It's likely that Mona's twelve-year-old had initially been drawn to Monk because he seemed to be a man who would care for her in the way Mona's father hadn't in that earlier scene and others. Each time Monk refused an important request, that exiled part's bubble of hope burst: "Monk is no different from Dad! I thought I was saved, but I'm still trapped back there, unprotected from my crazy mom!" If Mona can continue to show the exiled part that she can protect and care for it, it won't project all those expectations onto Monk and will no longer live in the past. Instead, Monk will be the beneficiary of that secure inner teen's irreverent sense of humor and cleverness.

The other aspect of Mona's account I want to underscore is that she used the fight with Monk to find and heal a key exile in herself. When partners can do this, they come to trust that such disconnecting episodes, as uncomfortable as they are, can be tremendously valuable opportunities to heal in ways that will serve the relationship in the future. For that to be the case, however, both partners must commit to the counterintuitive process of looking inside to change things when they are hurt by the other.

EXTREME BELIEFS ABOUT RELATIONSHIPS

Like Mona's twelve-year-old, exiles feel orphaned and rejected. They are desperate to be rescued from their wretched state and to be loved and healed. This alone means that exiles will powerfully influence your ability to be intimate. In addition, however, exiles carry a variety of extreme beliefs about what love is, whether they are worthy of it, who they must get it from, and whether it will last. Often they acquired these beliefs from experiences with caretakers during your younger years, but their extreme beliefs may also come from being burned later in life.

What Love Is

Many of my clients never or rarely experienced love from their parents. Instead, because of their parents' parts, the clients were objectified in some way as children. For example, if your father needed you to take care of him emotionally, he only valued the parts of you that could do that—caretaking, achieving, or sexual parts—and you had to exile your own vulnerability. To those exiles, love means taking on the overwhelming responsibility of trying futilely to take care of someone. If you were objectified in a sexual way by a parent, you will have exiles that believe love means danger and humiliation. If your mother couldn't stand for you to leave her, love means sacrificing all your hopes and ambitions for another person.

The point here is that many of our exiles are in a bind. They crave being loved but are convinced that love involves a great price. I have worked with many clients who, when they finally got close to a childlike exile, found that it was terrified or shut down. The part could not even trust the love of the Self. In these cases, it took many sessions in which my client was gently present with no pressure before the exile began to respond even slightly to the Self's love. Imagine how having such a scared and raw basement child, who thinks of love as engulfing or perilous, would impact your ability to be intimate with someone.

Unlovability and Survival Terror

In addition to having fears about love, most exiles also believe they are worthless or unlovable. If this is true of yours, it is usually because somehow they got that message from one or both of your parents. That message is terrifying to a child. The scariest message a child can receive is that they are not valued by a caretaker.

Children are born with a strong need for approval. There are good reasons for this. For much of our species' existence, most children didn't survive infancy due to illness or labor complications, as well as neglect or abuse. Even now, five million children die each year before age five. Human infants are high-maintenance organisms. They require constant attention and effort, remaining dependent on caregivers for an extraordinary period relative to other animals. For some, disapproval can equal death or extreme suffering.

Consequently, children are born with an overriding desire to be valued and an intense terror when they sense they aren't. What people call self-esteem is really a sense of security that one was valued as a child and is likely to survive. If caregivers seem to like you, you might make it; if not, you may be doomed.

These early survival fears abate when a child receives consistently positive messages about their worth and the safety of the environment. A well-nurtured child can ease into the world as if stepping into a warm bath. The parts of the child's personality designed to ensure survival relax and allow the child access to a rich inner life filled with wonderful sensations and resources. The more a child is able to intuit this inner realm, the more secure the child feels because, in addition to having access to more creative, adventurous, and playful parts, they will sense the Self—who they really are behind all the fear.

Children get the message that they are unlovable in three different ways. The first two happen when parents objectify their kids—view them as something other than who they are. Some parents objectify by conveying that their child is very valuable, even essential, but only in a certain role. Such parents treat their children as: surrogate spouses, confidantes, or lovers; trophies whose performance or appearance should enhance the parents' egos; sources of entertainment or distraction; saviors of their tenuous marriages; or allies against their enemy spouse. Children of those parents get the message that who they are is not valuable but that the role they are in is extremely valuable. Such children are in a confusing bind. They are often lavished with attention, special privileges, and praise. They come to feel extremely grateful and loyal to their parents. So why do they feel so worthless?

Children in the second group aren't confused at all about why they feel bad. Their parents objectified them as unwanted burdens that have ruined their lives, scapegoats for their own failings, targets of their displaced rage, or sex toys to be used and discarded. Often these children not only carry the embedded message from the parent that they aren't valued but they also blame themselves for creating the parent's behavior. They ask themselves, *Why would my mother be that way if there wasn't something wrong with me?* and conclude that there must be something wrong with them.

At least the children in the first group know that if they continue to play their role, they will survive. Children in the second group search desperately for a way to please but never can, or they give up and put a protective wall around their hearts. Consequently, their survival terror and sense of doom are pervasive.

The third way children get the message from parents that they aren't valued is by accident. It's so easy for children to misinterpret events and blame themselves. A child's parents divorce, and she assumes she must have done something wrong for her father to leave her. Her sister excels in school and gets lots of praise, and she concludes that she's not as valuable as her sister. Her brother has a chronic illness requiring a great deal of their parents' attention, and she feels abandoned and less important than him. When she hits preadolescence and starts to develop, her father suddenly stops hugging her, and she assumes that she did something bad. Based on my years of clinical practice, I have observed that unless parents are exquisitely sensitive to, and able to closely monitor and address, each child's reaction to family changes or traumas, it is likely that children will accumulate a sense of worthlessness to some degree.

How does your exiles' sense of unlovability affect your relationships? Of course, if you believe at your core that you are unlovable, you will have tremendous fear of having that confirmed by being rejected. As a result, some people don't take the risks necessary to find a good partner, keeping a distance from whoever tries to get close for fear that the other will see how vile they are. Other people become narcissists, constantly trying to fill their bottomless pit of worthlessness with the attention or accolades of others.

The Drive for Redemption

One other consequence of feeling unlovable deserves a fuller exploration because it is so pervasive and powerful. With the burden of unlovability comes not only survival terror, as mentioned earlier, but also an intense drive to be redeemed—to have the caretaker who originally gave you the message that you are unlovable change their mind and tell you that they do indeed value you. This drive for redemption will be a major factor in your choice of mate because you will seek someone who looks, sounds, or acts like the original redeemer. You will be strongly drawn to someone who has certain similarities to one of your parents, if that person was the original redeemer.

As you search for a partner, you will feel a big, intoxicating charge for certain people. If you follow that infatuated feeling inside to its source, it's likely that you will find one of those basement children in a state of ecstasy at the prospect of finally being redeemed and cared for in the way it has longed for. That particular person has become the exile's designated rescuer/nurturer/redeemer. The exile believes that if you can get that particular person to love you, it will prove that you aren't so unlovable after all. It will be as if your mother changed her mind and now finds you adorable, or your father not only stops viewing you as a failure but instead is very proud of you. The exile believes it will finally get the love and security it craved from their caregiver and will be pulled from the pool of shame and worthlessness in which it has been drowning.

Consider my client Tina, an attractive thirty-two-year-old veteran of the dating scene who came to me asking, "Why am I only attracted to assholes? Why can't I go for guys who respect me and treat me well?" After several sessions, Tina found an exiled part, an eight-year-old girl who was stuck in the past at a time when her father, whom she had earlier described as a demanding narcissist, was continually ignoring her attempts to get him to play with her. He was rarely home, and the little time he spent there was consumed with work or playing ball with her older brother. This younger version of Tina felt invisible to him, as though she didn't exist in his eyes. The little girl was staring desolately at her father as he played with her brother, waiting for him to notice her.

As she watched that scene from her past, Tina teared up and said she felt sad for that poor, ignored little girl. I asked Tina to enter that scene and be there with the little girl in the way she had needed someone to be at the time. Tina said she approached the girl and tried to get her attention, but the girl ignored her and kept gazing longingly at her father. I told Tina to hang in there and just keep showing the girl that she cared for her, even if the girl kept ignoring her. The girl looked at Tina curiously and told her that she only wanted her father. I had Tina ask the girl what she was afraid would happen if she didn't get her father's love. The girl said that if he didn't love her, there must be something wrong with her. Tina told the eight-year-old that there was nothing wrong with her and that, instead, her father just didn't know how to relate to little girls and thought boys were more important. The girl said she didn't care—she still needed his love to feel okay.

It took several sessions, during which Tina kept showing the eight-year-old she cared about her, for the girl to believe that Tina could offer her anything of value and to shift her gaze from her father to Tina. At some point, the girl dropped her stoic mask and fell sobbing into Tina's arms. When the girl was ready, Tina took her out of that scene to live in her apartment with her and continued to shower her with love. The worthlessness and unlovability lifted out of the little girl's body, replaced by a calm peacefulness.

Tina's father had given that little girl the burden of unlovability and, because the girl felt so bad, Tina had exiled her. Consequently, the girl didn't trust that she could get anything from Tina. Instead, she had Tina become infatuated with men who, like her father, were handsome and powerful but, also like her father, were self-centered workaholics. The pattern with these men was always the same. Tina would become totally enamored of each one, blind to his obvious red flags and thrilled with his attention because the eight-year-old felt suddenly released from the curse of unlovability and from exile. Tina would dote on the guy as if she were a grateful child. Gradually the man would complain of feeling smothered and would begin to treat her poorly. Tina would feel extremely wounded as the inner eight-year-old was thrust back into the rejecting scene with her father and enveloped once again in a black cloak of worthlessness. Frightened by the severity of her reactions, the man would either dump her or continue to mistreat her until her protective parts finally overrode the eight-year-old and pulled her out of the relationship. Then she would live with an abiding sense of unlovability until the next charismatic redeemer came along.

Once the eight-year-old started trusting that she didn't need her father's attention because Tina was there for her, everything changed. Now she could see the men's faults that had been obscured by the little girl's father trance. Now she was attracted to men who were interested in her and treated her well, even if they didn't look like male models and make six figures. She began seeing Steve, a divorced high-school teacher who was a devoted father to his two young sons. I continued to work with Tina as she tried to adjust to this new kind of man and new way of relating. She said that while she sometimes missed the rapturous early stages with the other men, it was a relief to be off that roller coaster and involved with someone who cared as much for her as she did for him. She also noticed that when Steve did something thoughtless, she didn't react with the same intensity. Tina's sense of worth no longer depended on her partner's actions because the little girl knew Tina loved her no matter what Steve did.

I have found that this drive for redemption has, to some degree, infected the love lives of most of my clients. It is reinforced by Western culture's relentless messages that finding that special person is the key to happiness and that to be alone is to be a loser. Just by growing up in this environment, you will have parts that won't let you enjoy life until you find that elusive soul mate and that are disinterested in anything you can offer them. If your parents injected even a moderate dose of worthlessness into such parts, you will be perpetually strapped into a worthlessness-driven roller coaster like Tina's or one of its many variations. There are many variations, one of which is the "tarnished halo" pattern in which you become dissatisfied when your chosen redeemer starts to like you ("She can't be that great if she thinks I'm attractive.") or shows parts of themselves that don't fit the redeemer's profile ("Why is he crying? He's supposed to be the strong one."). Another variation is the "dump before you get dumped" pattern in which you distance from your redeemer before they get close enough to see how defective you are.

The point is that unlovability and its associated survival terror and drive for redemption are powerful creators of the relationship hells we find ourselves trapped in. To deal with the burden of unlovability, our culture offers two doors: (1) find a redeemer to prove the unlovability wrong or (2) find activities or substances to distract from it (medication, TV, internet, work, shopping, drugs and alcohol, or other addictive behavior). Neither choice ever really works. The irony is that the effective door leads inside to the exiled childlike part that can be retrieved from the past hell in which it is stuck and shown by you that it never was unlovable in the first place.

Burdens from Abuse

Your designated redeemer will inevitably fail because they have no more idea of how to help that child out of the past than you do. Also, since you picked that person because they resembled the caregiver who hurt you, it is likely that they will, at some point, hurt you in the same way your parent did. It's as though you walk around with an invisible bear trap on your leg, searching for the person who holds the key to unlock the trap. When you find that person, you rejoice at the relief but later find that they carry other bear traps that they apply to both your legs.

If you were physically or sexually abused, your exiles will carry other beliefs about your value that contribute to these unlovability/redemption patterns. One such belief is that you brought the abuse on yourself and therefore you are bad and undeserving of real love. You will tolerate a great deal of abuse from your designated redeemer because it only confirms what you believe about yourself, and you will find it hard to trust or accept being treated respectfully. You will have parts that believe you have to pay somehow (perhaps in sexual favors or excessive caretaking) for any kindness you receive. You will assume that a decent person would never stay with you.

These are the kinds of assumptions most abused children make about themselves because their young minds can find no other explanation for why adults would treat them so badly. Also, it is safer for a child to hate themselves than to be angry at the abuser, who will only hurt them more if they show any defiance. If you were abused, it is likely that you have childlike exiles frozen in time when the abuse took place that hold fast to this kind of self-loathing.

These beliefs about unworthiness combine with an intense drive for redemption, the intensity of which is often positively correlated with the level and chronicity of abuse, to explain why so many people keep going back to abusive partners even when they have reasonable alternatives. They are addicted to the fleeting moments when the perceived redeemer shows them love or protects them, and they believe they deserve to be mistreated. It is important to remember that this is just a more extreme version of the redemption pattern that most people's exiles play out.

Whether Love Will Last

The final set of influential beliefs that exiles often carry has to do with whether they will lose whatever love they get. Some clients, when they finally make contact with an exile, see an image of a child who is shriveled, zombie-like, staring into space, and unresponsive to their presence. These parts have been so devastated by losing the love of a caretaker that they give up on ever getting any love again. The loss may have come from neglect, rejection, or abandonment by a parent, or from a sudden death or other situational loss. Those events, especially if they are repeated, leave a child not only with the assumption that love will never last but also with a conviction that the pain of losing it is so horrible that it is better to never open to it again. Such fatalism will keep you from risking true intimacy with anyone or, if you do take the risk of finding a partner, from ever really opening your heart to them. Because you expect them to leave at any moment, it seems wise not to invest much emotionally.

Self-Fulfilling Prophecies

These beliefs that our exiles carry about love not only limit how much intimacy is possible in our lives but also often create the exact scenarios that the exiles fear. For example, if you don't open your heart to your partner because you fear they will leave, they are much more likely to leave than if you did open to them. Once they do leave, your exile's belief is further confirmed, and you are more likely to create the same dynamic in your next relationship. As another example, if you become highly dependent on, controlling of, or codependent with your designated redeemer—because you feel so unlovable—they will lose respect for you and treat you poorly, confirming your beliefs about yourself.

It is one of the great injustices in this world that so often people who are abused as children are doomed to lives of recurrent mistreatment by the beliefs and emotions they accumulated during the initial abuse. Often such people are blamed by family members or mental health professionals for choosing and deriving pleasure from their plight. "There has to be something she's getting from being with such an awful guy. She must enjoy being dominated."

Exercise

You can get some idea of the kinds of extreme beliefs about love and relationships your exiles carry by thinking about your childhood, which is what many conventional therapies focus on.

For example, how much were you objectified, abused, or made to feel worthless by your parents? How frequently did you have to care for them? What might your exiles believe about love because of those experiences?

It is hard, however, to know exactly what your exiles' beliefs about love are until you actually listen to them directly. That may not be possible at this point because your protectors may not be ready to let you listen to them. In that case, this exercise will not yield much information, and you may need to find an IFS therapist to help you access your exiles' beliefs.

Think of times in your relationship when you felt extremely vulnerable. The feeling might be hurt, shame, fear of abandonment, fear of engulfment, rejection, neediness, or the drive for redemption. Choose the feeling that comes up most frequently. Now, focus on your memory of that feeling and see if you can sense where that part is located in or around your body. Notice how you feel toward that vulnerable part of you. Tell any parts that fear or dislike it that you are just going to get to know it a little better, and ask them to relax and step back. Continue to ask fearful or critical parts to step back until you feel curious about the exile. Once you feel purely curious, it's safe to ask the part what it wants you to know about itself. Try to listen with an open heart and mind.

If it feels safe, share what you learn with your partner.

ATTACHMENT THEORY AND EXILES

I assert a completely different explanation for why people abused as children often repeat the mistreatment in their current relationships. This dynamic relates to the power of the beliefs that exiles carry. To understand it, let's explore a body of research called *attachment theory*.

Decades ago, the founder of attachment theory, the British psychoanalyst John Bowlby, posited that early experiences with caretakers have a profound influence on people's later relationships. In the 1950s, Bowlby, after studying animals, proposed that human infants were no different from other ground-living primates in having an innate drive to become attached to their caregivers. He put forth the idea that the kind of attachment an infant forms to a parent will have a huge impact on their development. He suggested that a child will form an "internal working model" of the world based on those early interactions with a caretaker, which will influence the child's approach to life thereafter.

The psychologist Mary Ainsworth tested Bowlby's theory in the laboratory by separating infants from their birthing parent for twenty minutes and then reuniting them. She found that the kind of primary caregiver a child had was a good predictor of how the baby would respond to the separation, and that the way the child reacted—their attachment style—was a powerful predictor of success in later life. She distinguished four basic categories of attachment styles, a framework that has held up over hundreds of replications of this study. In the study, mothers who were consistently and tenderly responsive to their baby's needs produced securely attached infants. Those children showed signs of missing their mothers during separation and sometimes cried, but when the mothers came back, the children were quickly soothed and returned to their play.

Infants of mothers who were consistently cold, rejecting, neglectful, or rigid became avoidant. Avoidant children showed little emotion throughout, seeming indifferent to the parent's departure or return. Another group of mothers was inconsistent—sometimes appropriately nurturing and at other times trying to connect with the child in ways that were sudden and insensitive to the child's state of mind. Their infants showed what is called *ambivalent attachment*—they clutched at the mother when they were together, wailed inconsolably when they were separated, and remained that way after her return. The final group, those showing disorganized attachment, often were victims of abuse or of highly neglectful and unpredictable parenting. Those infants did strange things during the exercise, such as moving in circles, rocking back and forth, and entering a sort of frozen trance.

As my clients focus on the felt sense of their exiles, a visual image of those parts often comes to them. Over years of working with clients in this way, I have noticed that clients' images of exiles fit the same categories that attachment theorists use with children. That is, some clients see an image of a crying, needy boy or girl who frantically clings to them, much as ambivalently attached children cling to their mothers. Others find an inner child who seems totally distracted, unaware, or ignoring of their presence or angrily pouting and rejecting, like the avoidant children in the experiments. Still other exiles appear to be frozen, half dead, devoid of any life force, or in a kind of frenzy when the client first sees them, similar to Ainsworth's disorganized infants.

What Bowlby called the child's "internal working model" is the belief system about love carried by your exiles. There is considerable research in the attachment field documenting the impact of these working models on later relationships.

Attachment Reinjuries

The acts that created these beliefs and emotions in your exiles in the first place are called *attachment injuries*. When your intimate partner does something similar to what your original caretaker did, you suffer what I call an *attachment reinjury*. Attachment reinjuries, then, are events in which you experience your partner as having betrayed, abandoned, or humiliated you, reaffirming the original message to your exiles that they are unlovable. The degree to which that message devastates you depends on how much worthlessness your exiles already carry.

For example, Daniel and Sara came to see me because they both agreed that Daniel's explosive rages were destroying their relationship. They said that while he had always had a temper, things had become much worse since the death of his father two years earlier. Now, at unpredictable points in arguments with Sara, Daniel "just lost it" and, while he had never hit her, he became very loud and threatening, and he would follow her all over the house.

After a few history-taking sessions, I asked Daniel if he wanted to change the way that angry part of him took over, and he said he did. I had him focus on it and find where it seemed to be located in his body. He found it in his arms and fists. I had him focus on it there and asked him how he felt toward it. He said he was afraid of it because it could overwhelm him so suddenly and because it said and did such hurtful things. As he focused on it, an image appeared to him of a devil, complete with horns and a tail. With the intention of helping Daniel access his Self, I asked him to find the part of him that was afraid of that devil and see if it was willing to separate from him—to "step back" for a little while—so he could get to know this devil. He said that the part would only step back if the devil was first contained, so Daniel, in his mind's eye, put the devil in a locked room. As he looked at it through a window, Daniel said that the devil was furious at being locked up and was ranting and raving in the room. I asked how he felt toward it now, and he said he was interested in knowing why it was so upset.

The content and tone of Daniel's answer indicated that more of his Self was present at that point, which meant that it was safe to proceed, so I told Daniel to enter the room and ask the devil what it wanted him to know about itself. At first the devil was disrespectful, calling him names like "wimp" and "sissy," saying that he let people boss him around and that he was no match for Sara. It went on to say that Sara didn't care about him and cited as evidence the fact that she had gone on a business trip the week after his father had died.

As Daniel remained calm in the face of its ranting, the devil started to relax and told him how all Daniel's life, it had tried to protect him from attack and keep him from trusting too much. It said it had a "never again" philosophy in which no one gets a second chance to hurt him. I had Daniel ask it about the parts of him it protected. The devil showed Daniel an image of himself as a young boy in his parents' house, being berated by his father. Daniel watched this scene for several minutes, weeping silently through much of it. I had Daniel ask the boy if that was everything he wanted Daniel to know and if he felt as though Daniel fully understood how bad that experience was for him. The boy let Daniel know that that was one of many such episodes that left him feeling worthless. I had Daniel enter the scene and take the boy out of it to a safe, comfortable place in the present where he could unload that sense of worthlessness. Once in the safe place, the boy was able to remove the sense of worthlessness, which he experienced as a black tar on his skin. Daniel said that once the tar was off the boy, he brightened and wanted to go to the beach and play.

After Daniel helped the boy, I had him return to the devil to see how it reacted to this change. Daniel said that its image had changed and that now it looked like a teenage boy dressed in leather, looking tough but seeming much more relaxed. This devil-cum-teen agreed that if Daniel could take care of that boy, the devil wouldn't have to jump in all the time to protect the boy from Sara.

After watching Daniel do this work, Sara said she had more empathy for him and more understanding of what his rages were about. She also said she hadn't realized the impact of her leaving on the business trip and apologized. After several sessions like this, Daniel became far less volatile, and the focus of therapy shifted to other issues.

Daniel's exiles interpreted Sara's going on a business trip during his time of high need to mean that she didn't value him. To them, Sara was supposed to be the person who would remove their sense of unlovability, but instead she confirmed it by abandoning him. That slight ignited the shame and survival terror that Daniel's exiles already carried from his father's tongue lashings and made those young, needy parts of him even more desperate for Sara's love. But to Daniel's devil, she was no better than his father and, consequently, it would never again allow her access to those hurt little boys in Daniel.

Many couples enter my office embattled over seemingly petty issues. As therapy unfolds, however, it becomes clear that one of them suffered an attachment reinjury earlier in their relationship, sometimes even decades before. Some, like Daniel, felt abandoned at a time of great vulnerability. Others felt betrayed by an affair or terrorized by a physical threat or cruel comment during a previous fight. Whether or not you experience something your partner does as an attachment reinjury has less to do with the nature of the act and more to do with how much it reactivates the preexisting burdens of your exiles. Many people might have been disappointed with Sara but wouldn't have felt mortally wounded.

For so many couples, however, any awareness of the reinjury root of their squabbles is lost in the jungle of unpleasant and unrelated interactions that grow around it. Many therapists try to hack paths through that jungle—by teaching communication skills to couples, by helping them resolve the conflicts they bring in, or by assigning homework designed to create more intimacy—only to find that the paths they clear are quickly overgrown because the attachment reinjury that fertilizes the jungle is never unearthed.

On the other hand, once a couple gets close to that open attachment wound, the resulting pandemonium is often frightening to everyone, including the therapist. The reason couples do their best to avoid talking about attachment reinjuries is because the emotions surrounding such events have been so explosive in the past. The hurt partner feels so upset about the incident that their protective parts erupt in ways that, to an outside observer, often look like an extreme overreaction. The culpable partner becomes scared and defensive, minimizing the impact of their actions and focusing instead on the other's inability to get over it, which further enrages them, and so on. Because Daniel mainly feels his exiles' vulnerability, he has little awareness of how angry and demanding of an apology he is being. His constant harassment further enrages Sara, who responds by saying that she's not his father and he should get over it, and on they go. In other words, an attachment reinjury often sets in motion a process in which the injured partner repeatedly gets further wounded, and the perpetrator feels that they will never be forgiven.

Couples who get caught in escalating slugfests like that usually wind up in one of two patterns. One is to lock away the issue and try not to talk about it again. That solution can keep them together, albeit with increased protectiveness. Couples opting for that pattern come to have an exiled issue that affects them in the same way that an individual's exile does. It becomes an area of the relationship that they fear, and they avoid anything that might trigger it. Yet, like a child locked in the basement, they know it's there and needs attention. It's just that trying to deal with it always seems to make things worse.

The other pattern happens when they can't exile it. Like a missing tooth that your tongue can't stop returning to, the injured partner constantly brings up the issue, each time with the same painful result. These couples usually don't stay together. It is too stressful to live in that kind of crisis long-term. Obviously, neither of these patterns is ideal, but since most people have no idea of how to care and speak for their own exiles, they don't have alternatives.

Once a couple is able to unearth the attachment reinjury that lies beneath their daily jungle of charged exchanges, they have a chance to resolve it. A therapist who isn't intimidated by intense emotion can help the injured partner tell their story about how hurtful the other's actions were and help the other person listen compassionately and apologize sincerely. Couples can experience relief and renewed intimacy in such sessions that can serve them well for a time.

In my opinion, however, that healing is incomplete because while the injured person's exiles feel better about the partner, they still carry emotions and beliefs from earlier experiences that will be triggered again at some point. The couple has been brought back together after being blown apart by having stepped on a land mine, but their relationship remains a minefield.

Exercise

Have you suffered an attachment reinjury in the history of your relationship? How did you and your partner handle that event? Does it still come up or have you buried it? Which of your current conflicts might be related to it?

How scary would it be to follow the feelings from that event inside to find the parts that are stuck in those scenes and in much earlier ones?

TRAILHEADS AND TOR-MENTORS

This book will not only help you and your partner reconnect but also allow you to eliminate the minefield. To do that, you will need to be willing to find the ways your partner has hurt you and then use the feelings from those episodes as trailheads. What I mean by that is to focus on the hurt part of you and ask where it is stuck in the past. In doing that, you will be following the trail of emotion to its source—the original attachment injury—and in witnessing it, you will be able to heal it and learn to care for the exile that carried it. Later chapters will describe this process in more detail.

For now, know that it is possible to live with your partner in a very different way. When one of you gets hurt, you both focus inside, find the parts involved, witness what those parts want you to know about their current and past pain, and share your discoveries with each other. In doing so, you are clearing your minefields by stepping on the land mines each of you brought to the relationship and then defusing them so they won't explode again. By stepping on your land mines, your partner becomes your valued tor-mentor—they mentor you by tormenting you. Without them, you wouldn't be able to find many of the exiles you need to heal. And as you become comfortable speaking to them about your inner experiences with your exiles, after following the trailheads they reveal, you will find their loving acceptance and support sublime. Together you will share a vulnerable and rewarding form of intimacy as partners on a journey of mutual healing and growth. You will be helping each other find and rescue your basement children. Once released, those grateful, delightful inner children form a powerful bond between you that can override the typical irritations and differences that exist in all committed relationships.

SUMMARY

I'll summarize the points made in the preceding pages so we can examine each of them in more detail. First let's review why lasting intimacy is so difficult and elusive. Many of us have learned from our families and culture to exile our most sensitive and intimacy-seeking parts into the basements of our psyches. Because of having been exiled, those parts are love-starved. In addition, from our original attachment injuries, those exiles carry extreme beliefs about the kind of person who can save them, what love is, and what they deserve in relationships.

Because we don't know how to deal with our exiles, we enter intimate relationships hoping to get from our partner the love those exiles crave. Those basement-dwelling parts can make us pick the wrong person, make us become addicted to and stay with that person too long, and keep us from being attracted to or remaining with the right person.

Because our exiles are so desperate, easily hurt, and terrifying to us when they are upset, we have other parts that protect them by using one of the three projects: (1) changing our partner, (2) changing ourselves to please our partner, or (3) giving up on our partner and distracting or numbing.

Consequently, when our exiles are focused on our partner, the partner will feel overburdened by our clinging, jealousy, and neediness. Then when our protectors jump in, they will feel shut out and blamed.

When our partner acts like one of our parts, we will relate to them in the same way we relate to that part. If we judge ourselves as ridiculously weak when we feel sad or needy, when our partner's vulnerability triggers our own, we'll overtly or covertly judge our partner as weak. If we learned to view our assertive parts as selfish, we'll be uncomfortable with our partner's assertiveness.

SOLUTION

Now let's examine the solution to this seemingly impossible dilemma.

We each have a source of love within us called the Self. From this place, we can retrieve our exiles from our inner basements and heal their wounds sufficiently so that they trust us to care for them. When this happens, our protectors relax and cease to give our partner such a hard time. We can become our own parts' primary caretaker.

Because our former exiles are no longer locked away and now trust us, they are not so desperate, oversensitive, or in need of protection. They let us choose the right person and open our heart to that person without the neediness, trepidation, or protectiveness that characterized our former attempts at intimacy.

When our former exiles trust our Self to be their primary caretaker, our partner can be our parts' secondary caretaker and can help them feel accepted and loved by an outside person in a way they never have before. In that context, our parts can learn that intimacy can be safe and rewarding and that they deserve to be loved unconditionally.

When we love our parts and they trust our leadership, they don't have to distort our perception of our partner or take over and attack them.

They are free to care about our partner's needs because they aren't starving themselves. They can lavish our partner with affection because they have plenty to spare. Thus, the issues that most couples struggle with—expressing affection, respectful communication, and sensitivity to the other's needs—all flow naturally from a well-fed, Self-led inner system.

In addition to being the secondary caretaker of our parts, our partner can be an invaluable tor-mentor—that is, a person who mentors us by tormenting us. It is very difficult to find all our basement children when we're not in an intimate relationship because often we only become aware of them when they are triggered by an intimate partner. Inevitably our partner will act like an early caretaker who hurt us, and we will have an extreme reaction—an attachment reinjury. If we follow the trail of emotion to its inner source, we will find yet another exile in need of our love.

CHAPTER THREE

Courageous Love and Doomed Relationships

THE NEO-EXILES: PARTS EXILED BY THE RELATIONSHIP

So far we've focused on how the power and influence of the parts you exiled when you were younger and their protectors can organize your relationships. It is time now to discuss another set of parts that can make or break relationships. When he married, the writer Michael Ventura said this about his parts: "Some of them are gladly and enthusiastically married with, as the wonderful old phrase goes, 'abiding faith.' Some are married but frightened, nervously married, hesitant as to their capacities, their endurance. Some are hostile to the marriage. The frightened and hostile ones may be in the minority, yet they exist, they speak with our mouths sometimes."[1] The hostile ones are often the parts that had a great deal of access to you before you got involved with the other person but became exiled by your decision to become a couple with that person. I call these parts *neo-exiles* to distinguish them from the exiles you entered the relationship with.

Newlyweds Carlos and Marta were perpetually fighting over how much money she spent on clothes. When I had Carlos listen inside about that issue, he found a part that resented the fact that he hadn't gone out with his friends since their marriage. Once he spoke for that part to Marta, she said that she didn't like how much he used to drink with them, but otherwise she was fine if he went out once in a while. Carlos was surprised.

He had assumed that Marta hated his friends because of how upset she used to become when he'd return home. After Carlos's friendship-loving part felt heard by Marta and saw that she would make room for it, Carlos no longer hassled her about money.

In that example, the couple was able to accommodate Carlos's part because its exiling was based on a misunderstanding and Marta didn't have a big charge about the issues involved. This is not always the case.

Why are we so intent on getting our partner to change—to never show certain parts? There are many reasons. Let's start at the beginning—with the decision to commit to a partner. We already discussed how your basement exiles are looking for a redeemer who has qualities like the caretaker who originally hurt you or who seems strong and able to protect you. Those exiles will be upset when your partner strays from that profile, and you will try to get your partner to lock up the parts of them that don't fit your parts' expectations.

It's not true, however, that all mate-selection choices are made from those needy parts. If your exiles have been hurt repeatedly by intimacy, your protectors will override the exiles' redeemer search and begin looking for a partner who won't trigger your exiles. When you make a protector-based decision like that, you trade passion for safety and settle for a partner who may be boring but is, perhaps, conscientious, steady, loyal, nice, and so on. In other words, you have a partner who doesn't threaten your vulnerability or even want to get near it. In such an arrangement, whenever your partner strays from that safe profile, your protectors will punish them. To stay with you, your partner will have to lock up any parts that want intimacy or any communication that goes beneath the surface facade that initially attracted you.

In another protector-based scenario, you may have been drawn to your partner because you felt weak or incompetent and they seemed emotionally strong and sophisticated. As a result, whenever they show their own vulnerability or insecurity, you lose respect for them and let them know it in subtle ways. The partner quickly learns that their younger parts aren't welcome in your relationship. Because of our culture's socialization process, this pattern often, but not always, conforms to gender roles.

Some couples make it through the mate-selection process in a honeymoon state and just love everything about each other. That state only lasts until one or both partners' exiles get hurt or disappointed by the other. As we've discussed, it is at this point that their protectors initiate one or more of the three projects: change the partner, change themselves, or give up and distance. Each of these projects results in the exiling of previously powerful parts, whether they are yours or your partner's.

Perhaps your partner suddenly thinks your way of dressing is too casual, hates how hard you work, or is jealous of your friendships. Maybe they have trouble when you express vulnerability or neediness, or they can't tolerate your anger. Perhaps out of fear of losing your partner, you cut off from your sexuality, your assertiveness, or your passion for a risky career.

In this way, through your decision to become a couple, you wind up exiling or at least neglecting more parts, such as the ones that like to party, flirt, work, or couldn't care less about your appearance; or the ones that want nurturing or that want to speak about some imbalance in your relationship. Unlike the parts you exiled when young, however, these neo-exiles once had a great deal of power. They aren't used to being excluded, and they continue to have loud voices in your inner family despite their loss of influence. If, because of how you interact with your partner, there continues to be no room in your life for them, they can sabotage the relationship.

THE NEO-EXILING POWER OF ABANDONMENT ANXIETY

Many other reasons can also lead one partner to want to exile parts of the other, including differences in ethnicity, taste, class, upbringing, and trauma histories. One culprit, however, trumps all the others in its power to make one partner try to change the other, and that is abandonment anxiety. Since you have been socialized not to care for your own exiles and to believe that your partner holds the key to your happiness (if not your survival), you will try to eliminate or at least tame certain parts of your partner that become threatening. Ironically, it is often those same parts that attracted you in the first place. The sociologist Francesco Alberoni describes one version of this bind.

Whenever we fall in love, the other person always appears rich with a superabundant life. The beloved is always a vital force—free, unforeseeable, polymorphous. She is like a marvelous wild animal, extraordinarily beautiful and extraordinarily alive, an animal whose nature is not to be docile but rebellious, not weak but strong. The one we love attracts and gives pleasure precisely because she possesses this force, which is free and liberating but also unforeseeable and frightening. This is why the person who is more frightened imposes on the other a great many restrictions, a great many small sacrifices, all of which are basically intended to make her gentle, safe, and innocuous. And the other person gradually accepts them. She has friends, but she decides not to go out with them; she used to travel, but now she stays home; she used to love her profession, but now she neglects it in order to devote herself to her lover. To avoid upsetting her lover, she imperceptibly eradicates everything that may have that effect. She makes many small renunciations, none of which is serious. She gladly makes them because she wants her lover to be happy, and she tries to become what he wants her to be. Gradually she becomes domestic, available, always ready, always grateful. In this way, the marvelous wild beast is reduced to a domestic pet; the tropical flower, plucked from its environment, droops in a little vase by the window. And the lover who asked her to become like this because he wanted to be reassured, because he was frightened by the new experience, winds up missing in her what he had previously sought and found. The person who stands before him is not the same one he had fallen in love with, precisely because at that time she was different and fully alive. He asked her to model herself on his fears, and now he faces the result of those fears—her nothingness—and he no longer loves her.[2]

To translate that into IFS, suppose I have exiles that feel weak and worthless, and are stuck in a place of lifelessness. I fall in love with you—with your vitality, confidence, and independence—because you bring hope to my exiles of escape from their dreadful state. Yet because those parts of me feel so weak and worthless, and the parts can't believe my luck that someone like you would want to be with me, I constantly fear that you will find someone better and abandon me. Consequently, the same qualities in you that I so love become threatening, and my protectors go to work to erode your confidence, rein in your independence, and suck out your vitality. It doesn't take long for our relationship to become an arena for overt or covert battles.

The battles will be covert when, as in Alberoni's scenario, you succumb to my taming project and I succeed in neo-exiling all the lively parts of you. Those parts don't disappear, however. Instead, they commence an underground (unconscious) guerrilla war to fray our connection. You may find, for example, that for reasons you can't understand, your sex drive dries up, you develop an eating disorder or drinking problem, you become obsessed with work or the children, or you battle against a shameful longing to have an affair.

At the same time, my exiles fall out of love because this domesticated version of you no longer holds the promise of being able to pull them out of their pool of dreary worthlessness. Instead, I've managed to pull you into it. So I become critical of different things about you—your lack of desire for me, your drinking, or your lack of spontaneity or initiative, while I remain jealous and controlling, carefully watching to prevent your "marvelous wild animal" parts from returning to power.

If, on the other hand, your parts resist my project, ours will be an overtly rocky road. There will be lots of heated "Why are you trying to change me?" arguments. You begin "acting out"—having secret relationships and lying to me about where you've been, spending extravagantly, or otherwise loudly rebelling against my attempts to assert my authority. I, in turn, escalate my efforts to control your runaway train. I constantly monitor your activities, asking suspiciously about where you're going or have been. I become a relationship detective, checking your email and texts, combing through your credit-card receipts, asking probing questions when you arrive home late from your workday. I punctuate my simmering righteous contempt for your behavior with threats and ultimatums. And I hate you for forcing me into this role.

There are many different versions of this neo-exiling dance, all fueled by one or both partners' abandonment anxiety, which in turn is driven by a sense of worthlessness. As the author Laura Kipnis puts it, "We prostrate ourselves at love's portals, anxious for entry, like social strivers waiting at the rope line outside some exclusive club hoping to gain admission to its plushy chambers, thereby confirming our essential worth and making us interesting to ourselves."[3] The prospect of being abandoned is so daunting in part because, in our culture, being alone carries the stigma of being an unlovable loser. Anne Morrow Lindbergh describes this well: "How one hates to think of oneself as alone. How one avoids it. It seems to imply rejection or unpopularity. An early wallflower panic still clings to the word. One will be left, one fears, sitting in a straight-backed chair alone, while the popular girls are already chosen and spinning around the dance floor with their hot-palmed partners."[4] To avoid this plight, many people settle for dance partners they know don't fit well and keep dancing with them for years despite being miserable.

If Only We Weren't So Anxious

To avoid falling into the patterns described above, some partners try to exile their anxiety and become dominated by protectors that don't let them care deeply about the other or invest much in the relationship. *So what if they leave? I'll be okay!* With that approach, you won't wind up in the detective/controller role, and you'll likely have more power in the relationship because of the rule of least investment: the one who is less invested in the continuation of the relationship can control the terms of it. That is, by acting as though you care less than your partner, you can constantly stir their anxiety and keep them in line. The downside to this strategy is that you wind up numb, cut off from your heart and from your partner's love, so you're constantly dissatisfied—which, of course, only increases your partner's anxiety. And your partner resents your implicit threats.

In situations in which each partner has highly vulnerable exiles (starving basement children), the normal rhythms of relationship also spark the three exiling projects. For example, despite what you might have hoped for or learned from the media, a healthy relationship isn't one in which both partners are perpetually close emotionally. We all have many parts, some of which love closeness, while others need independence. Infant researchers have shown that this rhythm of closeness and distance exists even in interactions between parents and their newborns. Babies will interact playfully with a parent for a period of time and then will suddenly turn away and disengage, as if they need a break from the intensity of interacting. So, from the beginning, we exhibit this alternating rhythm in intimate relationships. Some parents feel rejected when their baby pulls away from them. When that happens enough times, the baby will shut down. The same thing happens with couples.

If, after a period of connection, your partner wants to do something separate from you and you interpret that as a rejection, they will feel misunderstood and will resent your exiling project toward the parts of them that need a little distance. On the other hand, if, after a period of distance, you view your partner's bids for affection as being clingy and too dependent, your reaction can start a vicious cycle between the two of you, as the parts of them that want connection feel unwelcome.

Exercise

What parts of you have you exiled
because of your relationship?

How has your abandonment anxiety or your other
burdens led you to exile parts of your partner?

How do you think those neo-exiles
affect your relationship?

COURAGEOUS LOVE

If only there were a different way to handle that abandonment anxiety than to exile it or let it dominate our relationships. What if we knew how to become aware of our essential worth on our own? What if we trusted that, no matter what our partner did (including abandoning us), we really would be okay (maybe not great, but okay)—not because we can cut off from our feelings but because we have trust in our own Self-leadership? This is a healthy solution to this human dilemma, and when you achieve a degree of trust in Self-leadership, you become liberated from these exiling dances. You can accept and encourage your partner to explore all of their parts because they don't threaten you. Your partner senses that acceptance and freedom, which feel wonderful and unusual to them. They come to trust that they don't have to protect themselves from you, and they keep their heart open. They relax with the knowledge that they can go where their heart leads them, even if that is away from you, and you will remain connected at the level of Self despite the lack of proximity. Ralph Waldo Emerson said, "The condition which high friendship demands is the ability to do without it." The same is true for high love—to do without your partner's physical presence, if necessary, because you support their life's journey, even when it departs from yours.

That's a Tough One for Most of Us

I remember how hard it was at times in my academic career when I was called upon to manifest such a selfless spirit. For example, there were several young, sharp psychology interns I mentored who, if after their internship they had remained with the institute I worked for, could have helped me develop the IFS Model and furthered my career. While their interests or family considerations were drawing them elsewhere, I suspected that if I worked at it, I could convince them to stay with me. In each case, I struggled to keep my parts out of their decision-making processes so they could find their own paths. I didn't always succeed, but I'm proud of the times when I did.

Those episodes produced major inner battles, and the stakes weren't that high. I knew I'd basically be fine without the help of those students.

How hard is it, then, to keep your focus on what's best for the other person when that person is your intimate partner, the one your exiles are attached to for their well-being and survival? Too often we succumb to the temptation to clip our partner's wings so they won't fly away from us. If the exiling projects discussed above don't work, we may have to escalate.

Stalking, intimidation, and violence are often reflections of the desperate lengths to which abandonment fear will take us. Or we can develop a debilitating symptom and use it to keep our partner shackled to us.

Maybe you're not afraid that your partner will leave you but, instead, that you won't be respected by other people because of the way your partner is. Their appearance, manners, sense of humor, line of work, or general lack of sophistication reflects badly on you, and you're sure you'll wind up in the wrong class of people or, worse yet, friendless. Similarly, it may be one or both of your parents whose respect you sense is waning because of your choice of mate. In this case, your abandonment anxiety is focused on peers or parents rather than your partner, but it is no less fueling of exiling projects aimed at the offending parts of your partner.

This is not to suggest that if your partner tells you they're thinking of leaving, you should say, "That's fine, dear—you do what you need to do." Or that if they told embarrassing sexist jokes at the last party, you should think *That's just the way they are* and let it go. It's important to speak for your affected parts and to request the changes in your partner that they want. But it's also important to explore their need for those changes to the point that you are sure they aren't motivated by the factors outlined above. Also, if you remain Self-led when making the request, you will convey respect for the part of your partner that, for example, wants to leave or told the jokes. You aren't asking them to get rid of the part but rather to explore whether there might be other ways to take care of it.

It is only when you are able to calm your abandonment anxiety by caring for the parts that carry it that you can truly love your partner because you can put their growth above your need for security. I call this *courageous love*. It is rare because Western culture, including many psychotherapies and spiritual paths, encourages us to exile, rather than embrace, those scared parts.

Courageous love may seem similar to the concept of differentiation that is promoted in some psychotherapies, but courageous love doesn't involve a heightened sense of your differentness or separateness from your partner. That rugged individualist type of differentiation is more likely when you exile your anxiety and become dominated by protectors in the way that many men in our culture have been taught to do.

However, it is true that because you are less anxious, you are no longer as reactive to your partner's emotions, and, consequently, you feel more separate in that sense. But when you have courageous love for your partner, at another level you feel more connected and similar to them than when you were anxious. You understand what the nineteenth-century philosopher William James meant when he said at the turn of the century, "Every bit of us, at every moment, is part and parcel of a wider self." You recognize that at the level of your Selves, you are not different because you are drops of the same divine ocean or sparks of the same eternal flame, part and parcel of the wider Self. It is this realization of connectedness that allows you to give your partner the freedom to grow. It is the same kind of love that a parent wants to have for their child, to let them follow their heart without undue concern for their needs and with an abiding sense of the parent's loving presence accompanying them even when they come to love someone else, adopt beliefs and practices that contradict theirs, or are geographically distant. Why is it so much easier to have this kind of love for your child than your partner? Only because you have been socialized to believe that your partner, not your children, should take care of your parts. When you become the one your parts trust and look to, you can have courageous love for everyone. Courageous love also means having the courage to love someone despite the potential for tremendous pain. Many of us who carry deep attachment injuries have protectors that see no good coming from allowing us to care enough for another person that losing them could hurt. These protectors have a variety of strategies designed to keep our needy, vulnerable exiles from fully attaching to our partner—to never let our partner fully enter our heart. The position of many protectors is that the more attached exiles become, the greater the pain when the inevitable end comes. To face the terror of that potential loss and open wide your unguarded heart takes considerable courage. You will not have the courage to let your parts strongly attach to another unless they are already attached to you. If your exiles trust that even if you lose your partner, they will have you to help them with the pain of the loss and to care for them in general, your protectors will open the gate. If that isn't the case, they won't allow the gate to open, and your prospects for real intimacy will be limited.

It's quite a bit easier to seem as though you have courageous love for a partner's growth if you never really let them in. If you don't let yourself feel much for another, you won't have that much to lose. The challenge is to do both—to love someone intensely and with abandon while simultaneously fostering their growth, even if it's away from you, and accepting their parts. Not many people can do that.

It's important to clarify that this discussion of courageous love is not a polemic against commitment. Instead, it raises questions regarding what you are committing to and why. Courageous love involves commitment to fostering the mutual exploration, healing, and growth of both internal families and Self-to-Self connectedness. You and your partner may agree that this process best takes place in the context of an exclusive relationship. Before many people can fully open their heart to their partner, they need reassurance that they won't be abandoned. Perhaps you have exiles that are so afraid of being hurt that whenever you begin getting close to someone, you lose your desire for that person and point your heart elsewhere. The Self-led vision of devoting yourself to one person allows you to follow the trailheads that arise when the usual escapes are eliminated. Or perhaps your exiles carry burdens of betrayal from previous relationships. Being with a partner who is willing to focus exclusively on you creates a safe environment for you to heal those parts. Or it may be that for other good reasons—sharing resources raising children, and sexually transmitted diseases among them—you and your partner agree that exclusivity is desired.

Mutual growth can occur in relationships involving agreements of exclusivity as well as those that don't, as long as the agreements are made from

Self rather than from the anxiety of parts. Whether that anxiety manifests as possessiveness or commitment phobia, it is no basis for a relationship.

I believe there would be far less fear of commitment if you could trust that you were committing to a Self-led relationship based on courageous love rather than to a process that requires the exiling of your exuberance. As the Jungian analyst Adolf Guggenbühl-Craig writes, "How often one observes how interesting, witty, and animated the married person is when alone, but then with the marriage partner present, every sign of liveliness vanishes."[5] That's a steep price to pay for the false security of parts-based commitment. Little wonder that so many make that bargain with great trepidation and break it at the first opportunity. The irony is that a Self-to-Self relationship based on courageous love is so fulfilling that if you were to taste it, you wouldn't be inclined to leave it. To have all of your parts feel accepted and embraced; to have the freedom to explore and express all of them so that your liveliness doesn't have to vanish; to experience abiding encouragement to follow your trailheads and learn your lessons; to know that the loving support of the other's Self is always there, no matter how life hurts you and no matter how the parts of each of you interfere; to feel the sacred "coming home" sense of connection to the divine in each other—for most of us, that is our heart's desire. Why would you want to leave that?

Finally, courageous love also applies to all aspects of inner and outer relating. Courageous love includes all of the following:

You love your parts enough that you speak to your partner for them even though your partner might react angrily. Many people sacrifice groups of their parts out of fear of upsetting or losing their partner. I often ask clients if they would remain silent if their external children were suffering in the same way. I encourage them to listen to and respect the needs of their parts as much as they would their children. Again, this is only possible if the parts that are attached to your partner trust you to care for them if they get angry or leave.

You have the courage to listen to feedback from your partner that parts of you may not want to hear. Your partner can help you learn the lessons you are here to learn by revealing trailheads you can pursue, and also by holding up a mirror and letting you know the effects of your parts on them. Most of us have little idea of the powerful impact our protectors have on others because when they are active, we're mainly feeling the exiles they are protecting. Seeing the value and truth in your partner's criticism can be challenging for that reason and, as well, because often they're speaking from a protector when they're criticizing you.

Your partner's extreme presentation makes it easy to write off what they're saying and miss the nuggets of truth embedded in their angry message. When you are able to listen with courageous love, you can hear those nuggets and then find and heal the parts involved in your triggered attitudes and behaviors. You also have the courage to apologize with an open heart and make a lasting repair.

When things get dark and both you and your partner are in a hurtful parts war, you have the courage to not activate the usual escape routes of rage, drugs, work, chronic distance, dreaming about or having affairs, and so on, and instead unilaterally initiate a repair process (discussed in depth later). Taking the first step away from protectiveness and toward vulnerability is a tremendously brave act for many people, and the reluctance to do it keeps many couples entrenched for extended periods.

You have the courage to drop all your defenses and totally open to your partner. You may remember the moments in your life when you felt fully yourself—unguarded and available—with another person. You remember them because they are rare and because they are so beautiful and precious. You felt unusually seen, known, and touched in those encounters because your protectors weren't screening out your partner's energy. Likewise, you extended an unfiltered love toward your partner. When you have courageous love, such encounters become much more common because the stakes are lower. If such utter vulnerability results in pain, you know you can handle it.

Exercise

Imagine that your partner comes to you and says with conviction and sincerity that they no longer want to be with you. Notice the parts of you that come up, both the protectors and the exiles they protect. Notice how they make your body feel. Separate from other parts until you feel curious about these. Find out about their fears and how much these parts trust you to care for them.

If you are aware of parts that are relieved or happy about the fantasy of your partner leaving you, try to be curious with them. Ask what would be good about that scenario. They may be the neo-exiles that you have sacrificed out of fear of losing your partner. Find out if there is a way you could better care for them even while you are with your partner.

DOOMED RELATIONSHIPS

Many of the couples I see in my office show no evidence of courageous love or Self-to-Self relating. Instead, they are dominated by protective parts that have them locked in tedious, predictable, and immature-seeming patterns that they themselves hate. Their interactions display the qualities that the researcher John Gottman calls "the Four Horsemen of the Apocalypse" because they hearken the demise of a relationship.[6] These Four Horsemen include criticism, contempt, defensiveness, and stonewalling.

Let's reexamine those four through the lens of IFS. The first two are the offensive weapons—the cannonballs that couples fire at each other's castles. Criticism is a complaint to which you add a message about your partner's character, such as, "You didn't empty the garbage today. Why are you so lazy?" Contempt includes sarcasm, name-calling, mockery, eye-rolling, and moralizing, all of which give your partner the impression that you are generally disgusted with them. Other related cannonballs include the more aggressive weapons of intimidation, such as threats of abandonment or violence. Criticism and contempt are the shame-based weapons used by our protectors when they take on the first of the three projects discussed earlier—changing your partner back into the person they were supposed to be.

The reason these weapons are so destructive is that they give your partner the message that they are worthless and that you are better than them. If they, like most of us, have exiles worried that they are worthless and unlovable, that message from you confirms their worst fears—that indeed they are worthless and unlovable.

That conclusion, in turn, arouses your partner's exiles' childlike terror that since no one will ever love them, they will be alone forever and may not survive. Their body is flooded with the physiological sensations of panic from times in their childhood when they were abandoned or rejected (attachment injuries)—times when it felt as though they might not survive. When their exiles are triggered to that extreme, their fight, flight, or freeze protectors automatically take over, further juicing their physiology and leading them to attack or defend in extreme ways. Gottman describes how, when partners are emotionally flooded like that, they can't pay attention to or take in what their partner says and are in a highly reactive, impulsive mode. In that state, trying to discuss issues is pointless because the person is bound to react with one of the Four Horsemen.

The other two Horsemen, defensiveness and stonewalling, are designed to protect your castle from your partner's cannonballs. Defensiveness is like the missile defense system that tries to intercept your partner's cannonballs before they reach you, while stonewalling is a dome of numbness you erect to keep them from penetrating when they do get through. Defensiveness and stonewalling are often used by protectors when they have adopted the third project of giving up on getting what they need from your partner.

The alert reader will have noticed that Gottman's Four Horsemen only cover the first and third projects that protectors adopt. What about the second one—changing yourself in order to get your partner to love you again? I believe that Gottman didn't include the behaviors related to that project—placating, obsequiousness, and self-criticism—because they don't necessarily portend the imminent doom of the relationship. Many relationships go on indefinitely with one partner playing the one-down role. The one-down partner pays a high price, however, due to being dominated by inner critics and having to exile so many parts.

Other patterns in couples, when the pair are not in overt conflict, may also foreshadow dissolution. For example, as you and your partner interact in daily life, parts of you are keeping track of the way your partner is relating, scanning for signs regarding how they feel about you—and your partner is doing the same thing. If, when you start a conversation, your partner ignores you or seems distracted, an internal warning light goes off until a later time when they seem interested or do something nice, and your parts relax again. If your partner consistently turns away from your bids for connection over an extended period, the inner warning light goes from amber to red. Looking to reduce your exiles' insecurity, you ask your partner how they feel toward you and are met with defensiveness or, worse, contempt for being insecure, and your exiles panic, sensing impending abandonment. Sequences like this cause the protective parts of you to move in and establish permanent residence. Once that happens, your relationship will manifest all the things Gottman says characterize couples in trouble: (1) the Four Horsemen when you are in conflict, (2) ignoring or rejecting each other's bids for connection in your daily interactions, (3) rejecting attempts to repair the relationship, (4) chronically describing your relationship negatively, and (5) highlighting the hurtful, stupid things your partner has done in the past.

This hijacking of your heart by protective parts manifests as a state Gottman calls "negative sentiment override," in which you never give your partner a break. In your mind, your protectors give their every action (even apparently generous or affectionate ones) a negative spin—they only did it because they know you'd be angry if they didn't, they're just trying to get on your good side so you'll have sex with them, and so on. Behaviors that, before the hijacking by protectors, would be mildly irritating become major transgressions afterward, and you come after them with both barrels blazing.

In addition, your protectors set up camp in your eyes, distorting your perception to the point that your once-attractive mate looks downright ugly. They can also dampen sensation, making you numb to their touch and taking any thrill out of your lovemaking. In general, protectors calcify your heart toward your partner, and even when you are not directly manifesting one of the Four Horsemen, you are obviously cold and distant, with a sour, disapproving energy seeping from your pores.

Thus, from the IFS perspective, Gottman's observations provide an accurate description of what happens when one or both partners' protectors decide that they've had enough and are through letting you open your heart enough to be hurt. People reach this point for a variety of reasons. Some partners come to the relationship with exiles that are already extremely vulnerable and protectors that are on high alert, so it doesn't take much for their drawbridges to go up permanently. Often it is a specific event along the lines of an attachment reinjury that arouses similar feelings from childhood carried by your exiles, which makes your protectors say, "Never again!"

For people whose exiles are not as delicate, more often it takes a cumulative series of hurtful interactions—continuous exposure to your partner's contempt, for example—that builds up to the "last straw" event. Or it might be that an event unrelated to the relationship, such as the death of a parent, triggers your exiles and sets off a destructive sequence of interactions with your partner, who doesn't know how to deal with your pain.

Or perhaps your hijacking is not related to being hurt by your partner but instead is an internal coup thrown by the neo-exiles—the parts that were exiled by the relationship. In other words, the parts that never wanted the relationship in the first place and had to be locked away when you committed to it finally stage an inner jailbreak and take over your central command. Perhaps those parts struggled for years to find a place in your life or to be accepted by your partner and finally gave up, deciding instead to wage a negative campaign against them.

Whatever the reason, when your or your partner's protectors take up permanent residence between you, they make couplehood a continuous nightmare because they do all the things Gottman describes. As a result, your exiles are constantly feeling rejected or abandoned, and you are always on guard. Physiologically, you are in chronic hyperarousal, a state that will lead to all kinds of stress-related health problems.

Exercise

What are your primary protectors relative to your partner, and which of the three projects do they favor?

Changing your partner through criticizing, contempt, threats of abandonment or violence, or inner grumbling about how badly your partner behaves

Changing yourself through self-criticism

Placating or being obsequious and overly caretaking or solicitous so your partner will love you

Giving up on getting what your exiles need from your partner through defensiveness and stonewalling

Dreaming of or finding another lover

Distracting or anesthetizing with such things as drugs, alcohol, work, TV, or the internet

How aware are you of the exiles those protectors guard? What are some of the feelings and beliefs those exiles carry? Common examples include: fear of abandonment; worthlessness and shame; extreme sense of physical vulnerability and terror; and a sense of incompetence, overwhelm, dependence, and neediness.

Have there been times in your relationship when your protectors took over so thoroughly that you experienced negative sentiment override? Were there times when you consistently rejected your partner's bids for affection?

Parts have tremendous power to affect your body, and it is important to help them find more direct ways to communicate. As you identify each of the parts above, notice where you find it in your body and consider the effect it has on your body—for example, what it does to your heart rate or breathing, your blood pressure or your ability to think clearly, and the general level of tension in your body. For each part, speak to it about that physiological impact and whether it needs to communicate with you in that way or whether you would listen otherwise.

THE PROS, THE ANTIS, AND THE UNAFFECTED

To better understand how this dynamic works, let's return to the single-parent metaphor—the mother with the basement children. Once committed to the Candy Man, the basement children were thrilled because they were going to get some food, but some of the protective children didn't trust the guy—he didn't seem to like them, and he was taking up their mother's attention.

To continue with this metaphor, still other parts might be like older children living away or cousins and other relatives whom this new commitment does not impact directly, so they don't have strong feelings about it. They are happy for the mother and support her decision as long as it seems good for her and the basement children. The mother then hears from three groups regarding this new relationship: the pros, the antis, and the unaffected supporters.

In the early stages of the relationship, the Candy Man is trying hard to please the mother and the basement children, so the disgruntled voices of the anti group are easily overridden by the happy pro group, who are supported by the unaffecteds. Once he starts ignoring or rejecting the mother's bids for affection, however, more of the unaffecteds begin to side with the anti group. Like the swing vote in an election, this shift of the unaffecteds can turn the tide. Before this shift, when your partner ignores your bid for affection, the outraged voices of the antis in your inner parliament were easily drowned out by the coalition of your pros and unaffecteds. "Don't worry about it—he's just had a bad day," they might say. Afterward, when your partner does the same thing, the antis have free rein, and their complaints are echoed by the unaffecteds, which together overwhelm the pros. When the inner swing vote shifts, your everyday attitude toward your relationship can suddenly change from one of happiness or contentment to resentment or intolerance. Your behavior toward your partner's bids for affection will change accordingly, and things between you can quickly spiral downward.

To change this negative override condition, Gottman prescribes a series of behavioral and cognitive exercises that target each problematic aspect of the relationship separately to help couples learn new ways of relating to each other and thinking about relationships. While I believe that such an approach can help couples become more aware of their toxic interactions and more focused on changing important patterns, it leaves their exiles unhealed. When exiles remain unhealed, it takes constant vigilance and energy to change patterns because each of you remains highly vulnerable and easily triggered. When exiles are healed, protectors naturally relax. Your sentries leave their posts, your castle walls crumble, and cannonballs melt; your exiles, newly liberated and emboldened, want to dance and play; and your Self-leadership is restored. In this state, you don't need to learn skills to avoid being contemptuous or closed off because you are naturally interested in and affectionate toward your partner, and you are able to negotiate effectively to find room for all your parts in your relationship.

In other words, improving relationships is not so much about bringing new skills or information into them as it is about healing the wounds that keep hearts encrusted and calloused. A heart, once opened and reenergized, already knows how to be loving and respectful. The trick is getting to the point where each partner feels safe to do that.

NOTICING PROTECTORS

In the list below, I combine Gottman's and my own observations about behaviors and beliefs that corrode relationships.[7] I encourage you to use the list to inform your parts detecting, which will help you identify manifestations of protective parts in yourself or your relationship that can be especially toxic. When you interact with your partner, you both can be watchful for the presence of those parts in your conversations and use those manifestations as trailheads—starting points for your inner work.

Here is a summary of common manifestations of protective parts that you can identify.

During conflict:

the Four Horsemen (criticism, contempt, defensiveness, and stonewalling—a.k.a. cannonballs, missiles, and domes)

intimidation attempts, including threats of abandonment or violence

ignoring or refusing to make repair attempts

feeling emotionally flooded

feeling numb and an absence of love for your partner

self-loathing and the urge to twist yourself into a pretzel to please or placate your partner

During daily interactions:

ignoring, rejecting, or not initiating bids for connection

chronic absence of sexual desire, affection, interest in being together, or intimate disclosure

chronic presence of urges such as bingeing, having an affair, shopping, sleeping, rage and desire for revenge, leaving your partner

viewing partner as unattractive and chronically focusing on partner's physical flaws

chronic presence of inner chatter, including:

>   self-criticism and fear of upsetting partner
>
>   overly caretaking of partner
>
>   feeling criticized or embarrassed by partner
>
>   strong and constant negative judgment toward partner
>
>   jealousy and distrust
>
>   desire to control partner
>
>   fear of being engulfed or controlled by partner
>
>   ruminating over previous hurts from partner and anticipating more
>
>   sense of being trapped and powerless unless partner changes
>
>   fear of being abandoned by partner

It's important to note that each of these feelings, beliefs, and behaviors is common at times in most relationships, so don't be alarmed if you're having some of these experiences. It's when these experiences become chronic and dominant that couples are doomed.

SUMMARY

Because we've covered so much territory, I will summarize the main themes before we move more concretely toward solutions. We have all learned to exile the parts of us that carry attachment injuries from childhood, including those related to traumas but also the parts of us that threatened or didn't fit into our families. These exiles carry extreme beliefs and emotions regarding intimate relationships and are guarded by other parts that protect them. We have been led to believe that our partner is the one who will, at long last, make our exiles feel good.

The above is a setup, for many reasons. First, not only can't our partner permanently unload the worthlessness and pain our exiles carry but, at some point, they are also likely to hurt us, by causing an attachment reinjury. Second, our culture is full of beliefs and forces that increase our dependence on our partner and constrain our ability to be fully present with them. Third, we often select our partner for the wrong reasons and from the wrong parts.

Inevitably, our partner hurts our exiles, which triggers our protectors to start one of their three projects: changing our partner, changing ourselves, or giving up. Because of those projects, as well as other reasons, we and our partners wind up with neo-exiles that resent being shut out of the relationship and try to sabotage it. After enough hurt, the protectors of each partner come to permanently dominate the relationship, and the couple enters "negative override." They no longer initiate bids for affection and reject any that are initiated. Their conflicts become characterized by the Four Horsemen of the Apocalypse: criticism, contempt, defensiveness, and stonewalling. The relationship is doomed.

There is a solution to this dilemma, and in the second half of the book we will get practical about achieving it. Thus far, I have hinted at this solution and will review those hints here.

It is possible to become the primary caretaker of your own exiles so that your partner is freed up to be their secondary caretaker. Everything improves once this has been achieved. To get there, however, both partners need to be willing to do a U-turn in their focus—from outside themselves to inside—and move from viewing themselves as having a unitary personality to the multiplicity perspective. Then you each can use the inevitable triggers that arise in your relationship as trailheads to follow inside and help the protectors and exiles you find there instead of taking up the three projects.

The trailhead-tracking process allows each of you to learn about what is happening inside when you are triggered—not just your initial protective reaction but also what's being protected and where it is stuck in the past (the original attachment injury). The next step—coming back to your partner and speaking for, rather than from, your parts—has two effects. First, since your partner isn't being directly attacked by your protectors, they can hear about your protective reactions from a place of respect and compassion. Second, your partner receives a more complete picture of their impact. Ideally, but not always, this picture includes information about your vulnerable exiles that were hurt by your partner and where in the past those exiles are stuck. It can also include information about any of your neo-exiles.

You and your partner can then negotiate changes—for example, ways to not keep triggering each other or to accommodate neo-exiles—Self to Self. When that occurs, you each can be clear about the changes you want in the relationship while remaining connected, even when dealing with difficult issues. As each of you feels safe to expose to your partner the parts you have hidden from the world, you feel embraced by each other, and intimacy and a sense of acceptance grow. In this state, you both feel free to spontaneously give and receive bids for affection. You don't need to learn communication skills—you will communicate skillfully and affectionately because your hearts are open and you have access to the qualities of Self, particularly curiosity, compassion, clarity, courage, and calm.

Of course, the process doesn't always go smoothly, and at times protective parts will take over and recruit some of the Four Horsemen to express themselves. That won't damage your connection, or will do so only temporarily, if two things are present. First, the receiver of the parts attack holds Self-leadership—in other words, knows that the attack is coming from just a part of their partner, comforts their own exiles, and, in the words of the IFS therapist Mona Barbera, "gives better back."[8] Holding Self-leadership in the face of your partner's extreme protectors is asking a great deal of you, however, and is unrealistic to expect consistently until you've done quite a bit of inner healing.

More often, you will also react from protective parts, and a "parts war" will ensue. There is no reason to panic when that happens because, in most cases, any inner damage to either partner's exiles is repairable. So the second requirement is that, later on, both partners are able to repair the damage, both inside themselves and with each other. In this next section, we will examine what that entails.

When all that is possible, you and your partner achieve what I call resilient intimacy along with courageous love. You also become each other's tor-mentor, helping each other heal by surfacing the wounds that need loving attention.

CHAPTER FOUR

An Example of Growing Toward Self-Leadership

THE KEVIN BRADY STORY

To illustrate the concepts I've discussed so far, let me introduce my client Kevin Brady,[*] who epitomized the American success story. Brilliant, charismatic, in command of himself, he was the head of a university hospital's trauma unit and a much-admired clinical professor at the medical school. While only in his early fifties, he published frequently in medical journals, and he had invented two surgical tools that were widely used across the country. His young residents were scared of him—he was known for his sharp tongue and for the fact that he didn't suffer fools gladly—but his trauma unit was the most respected in the Midwest. Everything at home looked perfect to outsiders. He was married to a bright woman with a career of her own, and they had two high-achieving children: a son, who played the violin in a respected local quartet; and a daughter, who had been accepted for early admission to an Ivy League college.

When we first met, Kevin had an intimidating air common to men who like to control conversation, especially when they don't know what to expect. Through well-timed pauses or disdainful looks, he quickly made it clear that I was to follow his lead. There's a whole butt-sniffing ceremony that takes place during first encounters between American men that's enhanced

---

[*] The names and details in this case have been changed. It is adapted from Richard C. Schwartz, "Don't Look Back," *Family Therapy Networker* (March/April 1997): 40–45.

when one is client and the other is therapist. Often I can enjoy watching the ritual, even as I participate in it. With the formidable Dr. Brady, I was too busy trying not to make a false move to be able to enjoy myself.

THE EFFECTS OF TRAUMA

Power-oriented protectors often belong to people who have experienced powerlessness, which brings us to the topic of trauma. To be fully present in the world, we need to trust that we belong in it—that our existence is supported by a higher power, the culture, and our direct caretakers. Different kinds of trauma will affect our trust in those three levels differently.

Unfortunately, the traumas inflicted by caretakers—whether active, such as sexual and physical abuse, sudden episodes of rage, threats of abandonment, and constant shame; or passive, such as neglect and abandonment—often make children feel vulnerable at every level. Nothing seems safe, so they can never relax their guard. These acts work to exile our vulnerable parts, and our lives become dominated by protectors that are emotionally frozen in the past during the trauma and take on the mantra of "never again."

Never again will these protectors allow the person to be that trusting, open, innocent, spontaneous, playful, or loving, which means never again letting the parts that contain those qualities see the light of day. Many traumatized clients are hypervigilant—their inner sentries constantly scan the environment for danger and overreact to anything resembling the original traumatic interactions.

"Never again" also applies to control. Traumatized people decide, often unconsciously, they'll never again be that powerless. For some, like Kevin Brady, that translates into constantly striving for control over the people and events in their lives. They are often high achievers who climb to positions of power and privilege from which they have the resources to make their lives as safe as possible. Others take control by avoiding people, hiding from a world that seems merciless. Either way, life is predictable, and no one gets close enough to hurt them. The boredom and loneliness of either kind of controlled life seem like a small price to pay to minimize the threat of reinjury.

Just as 9/11 changed America's perception of the world and the need to control it, those who are blindsided by abuse or neglect overbudget their own internal Pentagons to protect and control their little corners of the world. To these protective parts of them, their environment seems as dangerous today as it was when they were truly imperiled.

What happened to make Kevin feel imperiled? Kevin's father, a doctor in southern Illinois, had divorced Kevin's mother when the boy was seven, moved to another state, and remarried. After that, he neither paid child support nor saw his son. Kevin's mother, who went to work as a hospital receptionist, was preoccupied for much of his childhood with a series of unhappy relationships with men, one of whom sometimes hit her in Kevin's presence. Kevin, her only child, sensed that his mother often wished he just weren't around. Despite his father's abandonment and his mother's emotional neglect, Kevin threw himself into his schoolwork and earned straight As in high school. He silently vowed to build a life free of rejection and humiliation—and he did. He won scholarships and fellowships to an excellent college and medical school, and he never looked back. After he married, Kevin never expressed resentment about the difficult circumstances of his upbringing. He seemed to be one of those people who are just born resilient.

Kevin prided himself in being brutally honest with people, yet he was a master of denial. He might be able to tell someone off, but his background had forced him to deny or minimize the existence of any emotions other than anger. The cultural anthropologist Ernest Becker wrote, "A full apprehension of man's condition would drive him insane."[1] Kevin and many people like him believe that if they ever fully appreciate how bad their childhoods were, they will go insane—never stop crying, be unable to work, or have a "breakdown."

KEVIN'S PROTECTORS

In that first session with Kevin, I speculated to myself about the parts of him that were addressing me. There was clearly a controller that strived to dominate relationships and keep people distant with aloof arrogance, a sentry that was scanning me for danger, a perfectionistic worker that made him so successful, and a part that denied any problems except that his wife was very upset with him.

Two weeks before that first session, Kevin's wife, Helen, had had it. For more than thirty years, she had endured his carping about her taste in clothes, her child-rearing, her political opinions, her education, her intelligence, and her logic. She was sick of his long hours at work and his failure to be available to her. She never knew when he'd come home in a dark mood, making her and the kids feel that, for their own good, they'd better tiptoe around. She'd had it with being interrupted contemptuously at dinner parties and dismissed in public as stupid. She'd watched their children come home with handfuls of As and seen how Kevin concentrated on the one B. Now that their younger child was about to graduate from high school, she felt free to start working full-time and putting her money in a separate account. She wasn't taking any more of his crap—if he didn't change, she was going to leave him. She knew these parts of him much better than I did.

All that crap—the sniping comments, perfectionism, defensiveness, workaholism, and moodiness—came from Kevin's inner protectors, which were just doing their jobs. Never again would they let Kevin get hurt, even if it meant hurting others. They had no choice but to continue protecting him until he was less vulnerable. For Helen or me to point out the error in his ways was worse than futile; it only made him feel ashamed and all the more defensive. I would have to find a way to be allowed past the guards.

CRACKED FORTRESS

While Helen's attacks on Kevin's character were backfiring, her new commitment to leaving wasn't. A Leonard Cohen song goes, "There is a crack, a crack in everything. That's how the light gets in."[2] Helen's threat opened a few cracks in Kevin's fortress, but it was not yet clear how much light would get in.

Faced with Helen's ultimatum, Kevin agreed to come into therapy, but after a few marital sessions, he asked to see me individually. Once alone with me, he said he didn't think much of psychotherapy, nor of emotions in general, and he couldn't understand why she was so sensitive. Sure, he had high standards; he said he was harder on himself than anyone else and owed much of his success to it. He admitted that he was sometimes testy and judgmental but claimed that it came with the territory of a high-pressure job like his. He said his ability to find a fatal flaw in a workup was legendary among the residents, and while it didn't win him friends, it earned him respect and sometimes saved lives. Similarly, he didn't need his kids to love him, just to respect him and his advice. Then, with an unexpected shift in tone, he said he was terrified that Helen really would leave him. He didn't know how he'd survive without her. An exiled part of Kevin had found a small crack and peeked out.

I sensed how rare and disorienting it was for Kevin to feel, much less show, that kind of vulnerability. I wanted to make that exiled part of him feel welcome and safe with me, but I knew my own protectors well enough to trust that his were watching my every move. Like mine would have been, Kevin's managers were undoubtedly terrified that I would exploit his openness somehow and were condemning that exiled part for giving me power over him. I had to be very careful in how I responded.

When Kevin opened that one small crack in his imposing fortress by telling me he feared the prospect of Helen leaving him, I knew better than to try to pry it further open. Instead, I tried to put his vigilant managers at ease by stressing how understandable that was and how devastated I had been when partners had left me. I then left that touchy subject and asked how it felt to him to be in therapy with me. I told him I had trouble showing any flaws or vulnerabilities to other men, and I wondered how it was for him. He replied that there were very few things he was afraid of but conceded that it was uncomfortable to be in this position with me. He didn't like to ask for help from anyone and prided himself on his independence. Nonetheless, things were not good at home, and he was in constant distress about it, so maybe I could help. The crack was widening on its own.

PROTECTOR FEARS

For the next six sessions, Kevin and I made a steadily growing list of his fears of revealing himself to me. He worried that he might cry, something he hadn't done since he was a boy. He warned that he didn't want to try some stupid New Age gimmick and would rather engage in some form of empirically verified therapy. He expressed contempt for victims who whimpered, whined, and blamed their parents or society for their problems; he was determined he wouldn't turn into one. He was afraid I might think less of him if he spoke of inner pain. He wasn't sure what was inside and argued that it was probably nothing important. Some things had happened in his life, he said, that he didn't want brought back. He feared falling into a black hole.

I took all his fears seriously, especially the one about falling into a black hole, which usually means being submerged in a pool of pain and shame. I told him that while we might encounter some parts of him that were hurting from events in the past, there was a way to help them heal without letting them take over. This might entail some crying, I said, but they would be tears of compassion, and they would be temporary. We could unload his pain so he would no longer have to fear that black hole.

But it was totally his choice. I assured him that I would never pressure him to do it, and if he chose not to, I would completely respect his decision. Because of my own experience, I understood what a scary prospect doing that inner work can be.

What I said to Kevin is true—I do understand. After a lifetime of avoiding my pain, I moved toward it kicking and screaming. And I only went there because, like Kevin, I was being consumed by it anyway. A situation had cracked open my own protectors' fortress and, like him, I could no longer contain feelings I had exiled since childhood. And I was a therapist who encouraged others to work with their emotions.

This was a much bigger challenge for someone like Kevin, who had steered his life far away from positions that might stir vulnerable emotions. While he witnessed a great deal of pain in the emergency room, he had been trained not to experience it for fear of losing clinical objectivity. He viewed himself as working in a war zone and took on the air of a stoic military commander. Feelings were not something he wanted in his work nor in his personal life.

I'm sure I traumatized my therapist during the sessions following the initial exposure of one of my exiles. I was convinced she'd lost respect for me and grilled her on what she thought of me. Since I was an experienced therapist, I also let her know what I thought she was doing wrong and told her I didn't think she was strong enough to work with me. I was an obnoxiously resistant client. Fortunately, she was patient with my inner guardians, giving them the reassurance and control they needed. Ultimately she passed all their tests, and they backed off and opened the gate. I let her accompany me on a painful journey into the land of my exiles.

This experience made me quite willing to give Kevin plenty of time before he decided whether to allow me to accompany him. I was happy to let his managers take whatever time they needed to sniff me out thoroughly and to know what they were getting into. It was their duty to protect him, and they had every right to challenge me until they felt satisfied that I wouldn't cause more damage—and might even be helpful.

GOING INSIDE

In one session, I asked Kevin to relax, close his eyes, direct his attention inward toward his critical thoughts, and ask what they were afraid would happen if they stopped harshly judging him and others. Kevin's first response was that he felt stupid talking to himself like that. Even though it seemed silly to him, I asked that he just try it as a simple experiment—as a way to get better acquainted with his thoughts and feelings. Reluctantly he proceeded and, with a look of serious concentration, he was silent for perhaps thirty seconds. Then Kevin said that he heard the words *I would be hurt.* "But that's crazy," he said. "How could being so judgmental protect me from being hurt?" I told him to ask that question inside; eventually his inner critic replied that if he criticized others, they wouldn't get close enough to hurt him. If he attacked himself, he would strive so hard and be so perfect that no one else would criticize him. I asked Kevin if he could thank this part for protecting him. When he did, he said he sensed what felt like the loosening of a band around his head.

I had Kevin ask this critic who it protected. He immediately saw in his mind's eye a large wall with a thick, heavy door, and he heard an inner voice saying that his pain was kept behind it. I decided to slow down. We had come to the threshold of his pain containment. I wanted to be certain we had full permission to proceed. Kevin and I spent two more sessions discussing whether it was safe to move toward his pain. We went over each of his fears once more, and I discussed how we could handle each one. I then had him refocus inside and ask if any parts objected to our moving forward. He said he didn't hear anything. We touched base with the critic once again and that part gave its permission for us to proceed. We would return to the door in the following session. It felt as though we were about to enter the abyss.

THE SUICIDAL PART

But, of course, it wasn't that easy. Kevin came to the next session saying he'd been feeling suicidal all week. He said that for as long as he could remember, the thought of suicide had lingered in the back of his mind; it was actually comforting in a way but had only become the strong urge he felt now on a few other occasions. He'd never acted on that urge but now was openly frightened that he would. I helped him reassure the parts that were so afraid of the suicidal one that we could release it from that role, after which they granted permission to work with it.

Schwartz: Go ahead and focus on that suicidal voice. Let's start with it in a room by itself, and you're outside the room.

Kevin: Okay, it's in the room.

Schwartz: How do you feel toward it?

Kevin: I'm relieved to have it locked up. It's very scary, with a black hood and all that.

Schwartz: Ask the parts that fear it to step back and let you and me get to know it. Tell them we won't go in the room until they think it's safe to do so.

Kevin: They don't want me to get to know it. They want to keep it locked up.

Schwartz: That's understandable, but our goal is to help it out of this scary role so they won't have to fear it so much. But we can't do that if they make you so afraid of it.

Kevin: They'll move back and watch, but only if they can jump back in any time.

Schwartz: That's fine. How do you feel toward the suicidal part now?

Kevin: (Calmly) I want to know why it would want me to die.

Schwartz: Go ahead and ask that from outside the room.

Kevin: It says that I deserve to die.

Schwartz: Ask what it's afraid would happen if you didn't.

Kevin: It says that I'll keep hurting people.

Schwartz: So it's trying to keep you from hurting people, is that right?

Kevin: That's what it says. But I help people. I'm a doctor, for God's sake!

Schwartz: Ask the part that's defending you now to step back. Then ask what that hooded guy wants to show you about hurting people.

Kevin: (After a long pause) I see myself yelling at my mother, and now she's crying.

Schwartz: How old are you?

Kevin: Seven or so. My father has just left us. I'm blaming my mother for making him leave, and she's destroyed.

I should never have done that. I'm afraid she's gonna leave now, too.

Schwartz: How do you feel toward that boy?

Kevin: (Crying softly) I feel so sorry for him. No wonder he decided he'd rather die than upset her again.

It's not uncommon for clients, upon reaching the brink of exile territory—which often appears to them as a wall, a cave, or an abyss—to experience a sudden escalation of protector activity (in Kevin's case, a suicidal part). They might go on some kind of binge, start cutting themselves, become enraged at me or someone else, or have a strong desire to stop therapy, leave town, or leave in the way Kevin wanted to. The severe symptoms used to scare me. I'd think the client was more disturbed than I'd originally believed. I'd have them evaluated for medication or hospitalization. I'd back away from exile territory.

Now I've come to expect such episodes and sometimes even predict them to clients. They are a natural, last-ditch reaction to the prospect of going where every part fears to tread. They also serve as a final test of the therapist's ability to stay present and not panic. When I can do that, things usually go the way they did with Kevin's suicidal part. This is not to suggest that medication or hospitalization aren't sometimes needed—only that it's important to consider the context in which symptoms arise and to not overreact.

HELPING EXILES HEAL

After connecting with his suicidal part, Kevin returned to the door to his pain. Fortunately for Kevin, he came to me after I had learned how to help exiles heal safely. After trying to help exiles and finding that clients sometimes had frightening backlash reactions later, I became much more cautious. I had to find a way to help clients get close to their exiles without being totally engulfed by them—because that was what the managers feared most. It turned out that the solution was one of those obvious things that's so simple you never think to do it. You can just ask exiles not to overwhelm your internal system with the emotion they hold as you approach them.

Parts can control the degree to which they blend their feelings with a person. Like prisoners in a castle, exiles try to rebel whenever cracks open in their captor's fortress. They don't think there's any other way to get help. But when they trust that we're coming to help them, they don't have to overwhelm and can allow people to get quite close without totally blending. Then clients will be able to feel exiled emotions but not to the extent that doing so threatens the system.

Once I figured that out, it became possible for clients to come close to, and then stay present with, a part long enough that it came to trust that the person cared about it. In some cases, that took quite a bit of time, and we'd spend a number of sessions just comforting a part.

From outside the door, I had Kevin ask his pain if it was willing to not overwhelm him once he entered and approached it. He heard a voice whisper okay. He went through the door and saw a seven-year-old boy curled up and shaking about ten feet from him. His first reaction was one of revulsion at the boy's weakness, but after I asked him to find that disgusted part and get it to step back, he quickly felt sad for the boy, although he didn't know why the boy was so upset. I asked Kevin to show the boy that he felt sad for him and cared about him. After some coaxing, Kevin was able to get the boy to sit up and even let Kevin put his arm around him. I was impressed at how this outwardly tough, cold man seemed to know just what to do to nurture the boy. By the end of that session, the boy said he'd begun to trust that Kevin cared about him. He asked, however, that Kevin spend time with him every day. That request triggered some of Kevin's protectors, who said that just as they thought, the boy would take all his time and energy, and he wouldn't get anything done. However, they reluctantly agreed to let him try it for a week.

At the next session, I was surprised that Kevin had kept his promise to the boy, spending five minutes with him each morning and also thinking about him occasionally throughout the day. The boy seemed very happy with this, as well as surprised. The first time they try to stay with exiles, many clients forget (or, more accurately, their protectors make them forget), and the parts feel abandoned. Kevin said he'd had strange dreams that he didn't remember and felt like being alone a lot. I told him that was par for the course during this period of therapy.

I asked if he was ready to see what the boy needed to show him about the past. He said yes, and I had him ask the boy to show him. He immediately saw himself as a seven-year-old boy curled up and shaking in a cardboard refrigerator box in his backyard. His parents were in the house fighting, and he could hear their shouts echoing through the windows. He had been inside the house watching them fight, his parents oblivious to his terror, until his father had hit his mother and she had screamed that she was leaving him. Kevin had run outside to hide and had lain shaking in the box for hours until they finally found him. This was one of many scenes of a childhood rife with betrayal, neglect, and horror that Kevin witnessed. At first, he would watch for a while and then shrug the scene off, saying something like, "So I was hurt—so what? Everybody gets hurt, many people much worse than this." At other times, he would explain to me why his mother or father couldn't have done any better than they did, as though apologizing for them. I asked him to find the parts that were saying those things and interrupting the witnessing of the young boy's pain, and to ask them to temporarily move to another "room." We would check back with them later.

Without that interference, the witnessing went more smoothly. Shortly after the fight, Kevin's father had left the family and never looked back. His mother went through a series of men, one of whom beat her in Kevin's presence. He sensed that she often wished he weren't there, and this realization, combined with a feeling of worthlessness due to his father's abandonment, produced a belief that if he depended on people or got close to them, he would be rejected or abandoned. His critic pledged "never again" and prodded him to excel academically. He soon found that he could lose himself in school and gain power over others through his brilliant academic performance.

These scenes of childhood pain that Kevin watched were not events he had repressed or forgotten but rather had held at arm's length. Now he watched as though they were very emotional, richly detailed scenes from a movie. On occasion, he felt so sorry for the hero of that movie that he did indeed weep with compassion. After each scene, he embraced the young boy in them and thanked him for showing him what had happened. He then asked where in his body he carried the feelings or beliefs from those events. The seven-year-old carried a ball of burning fire in his gut, which Kevin helped pull out of the boy's stomach and threw to a healing place beyond his internal horizon. It returned moments later as a blue sapphire that the boy could wear over his heart. Then Kevin helped the lost boys find safe and comfortable places to stay in his inner world. One of them chose a sunlit room with easy access to a garden full of trees to climb. Kevin pledged to take better care of them in the future and to comfort rather than isolate them if they felt hurt by something that happened in the outside world.

This process of identifying and releasing the extreme emotion or belief that a part carries is called *unburdening*; in IFS, it is equivalent to healing the part. This is because once parts unburden, they often immediately transform into their naturally valuable states, as if released from a spell. When exiles such as Kevin's lost boys unburden, they become far less vulnerable, so their designated protectors can drop their guard and find new jobs.

With each new unburdening, Kevin's once-scathing inner critic relaxed and gradually took on the new role of career advisor. It remained an acute judge of quality, but instead of attacking his or other people's imperfections, it cheered him onward. He also found an end to his years of struggle with tension headaches as the critic's band around his head melted.

The unburdening and transformation of exiles allows the protective managers to relax, making the person less vulnerable to attack. Before this work, if anyone, but particularly Helen, was critical of Kevin, not only would he experience the discomfort of having someone upset with him but that criticism would be embellished by his own inner critic and would also fall like a depth charge into his resting pool of shame and humiliation. The pain of the present slight would be amplified by how it reverberated with all the past pain his parts still carried—his attachment injuries. As we pumped out Kevin's pool of pain, present-day criticisms lost their charge for him. The same was true with Helen's threatened abandonment. It no longer brought forth the physiological desperation—shaking and nausea—that it had earlier because it no longer sucked him back to the time when his father left. In addition, his young parts now knew that if Helen deserted them, Kevin would still be there for them. He had become their primary caretaker.

Kevin said he felt more peaceful inside, as though he was no longer trying to constantly stay one step ahead of something. He saw his mother differently—as a woman who could never feel loved and who never believed she deserved it—and he no longer felt the pent-up rage toward her that had plagued their relationship since his adolescence. He said that he'd spent his adulthood trying to let go of his past, and it seemed ironic to him that in order to do that, he had to get closer to it. That does seem ironic, and it's a hard sell for many people. Kevin finally took the full look that's required to be more present—having with him more parts that weren't stuck in the past or scared about the future.

HELEN'S WORK

So far, I have focused this story on my work with Kevin, both because I spent many more sessions with him than with Helen during this period and because the work with him was so illustrative of the kind of reconnection with exiles that is necessary for couples work to succeed.

Helen and I had several individual sessions as well, during which she followed the abundant trailheads that Kevin's contempt, workaholism, and distancing afforded. As one might guess, she found exiled little girls that were desperate for her distant father's affection, furious protectors that guarded those vulnerable exiles, and the caretaking part that had dominated her life for a long time and was currently held at bay by the angry parts. As her basement children came to trust her to care for them, her protectors' rage abated and they let her Self lead more in her interactions with Kevin. This didn't mean that she suddenly became nurturing and receptive toward him. Instead, she drew on other qualities of Self-leadership, including clarity, courage, and confidence. In our couples sessions, which were interspersed occasionally among the far more numerous individual ones with each partner during this initial phase of their therapy, she became increasingly able to speak in a calm and convincing way of her commitment to never again put herself at the mercy of Kevin's protectors. She was able to be forceful without being contemptuous and clear without being unkind, both in sessions and at home.

Whereas Helen's rageful part had terrified Kevin, her new strength attracted him and made him even more afraid of losing her. That not-unrealistic fear also kept him motivated to keep working with his parts, even when coming to see me was the last thing he wanted to do. Also, because he felt less bombarded by her rage, it was easier for his protectors to let us focus on his issues rather than on what she was doing to him and how she needed to change.

THE COUPLES SESSIONS

As Kevin and Helen each became more Self-led, we began to shift toward doing more couples sessions interspersed with occasional individual ones. When, as with the Bradys, a couple is initially so polarized that they cannot control their parts in the presence of the other, I move gradually from working with each partner separately to conjoint sessions. I find that letting couples activate each other in sessions is not only futile but can be harmful, as each partner's exiles become increasingly hurt and their protectors more extreme. Some highly conflictual and embattled couples don't need separate sessions because, despite their intense feelings, their parts trust them enough to step back and let them relate Self to Self in sessions. When that is the case, they often feel safe enough to expose their own vulnerability in the presence of their partner, so I don't have to split them up. Some of those sessions involve my working with one partner, in the way I did with Kevin, while the other watches. This can have a profound effect on both people.

Intimacy can deepen enormously when one person exposes parts that they feel ashamed of to another, especially when the other person can remain Self-led. If the witness accepts and offers love to the revealer, the revealer feels tremendous relief and delight at having something shameful accepted and feels grateful to the witness. The witness feels greater empathy for the revealer and feels privileged to be allowed into the revealer's inner sanctum.

This bonding increases whenever any previously hidden part is brought into the stream of love created by Self-to-Self connectedness. And it's particularly true for those parts we feel most ashamed of or think the other person disdains the most. If Helen had been in the room when Kevin found his seven-year-old in the refrigerator box, under normal circumstances she likely would have been deeply moved and would gain a new understanding of Kevin's distancing and criticizing that had bothered her so much. If she conveyed to Kevin her empathy for that boy and her new awareness of why he was the way he was, Kevin would feel seen and loved in a way he never had before.

I have been privileged to facilitate that kind of process innumerable times, and it never fails to move me to tears. Like many precious things, however, it is delicate, and care must be taken to ensure that it works. In the early stages of the therapy, there was no possibility that Helen could have witnessed from a Self-led place and no possibility that Kevin would have allowed himself such vulnerability with her in the room. Helen's protectors had only recently succeeded in overthrowing her caretakers, and they weren't about to let her open her heart to him until they saw big changes. Kevin's protectors were terrified of Helen's and wouldn't drop their guard in her presence. If, out of desperation, he had been that vulnerable in front of her, his seven-year-old would have been devastated when she responded from her cold and critical parts, whether in the session or at home. His protectors would attack him for ever allowing such openness and would vow never to let it happen again.

So the timing of when to encourage couples to be vulnerable to each other is crucial. I have learned the hard way about the powerful setbacks and backlash generated when partners are encouraged to do so prematurely. When I'm not sure if they can witness from Self, I'll err on the side of caution and help both become better able to caretake their own parts before asking them to witness each other's.

Once Kevin and Helen had reached the point where I sensed that if one of their parts took over in a session, I could get them to return to Self, I increased the couples sessions. In the beginning we talked about the issues they were facing—the separation, the kids, money. I asked for their permission to play "parts detector"—to stop the action when I noticed a part take over either of them and have them both focus inside on the protectors that were triggered.

BEING THE "I" IN THE STORM

When you are speaking with someone who triggers intense emotion, you usually don't have the luxury of following that trail inside to discover and heal your exile. Instead, you have to deal with the person in that moment despite what feels like an inferno in your gut, a huge boulder on your chest, or an explosion in your brain. You have to stay calm even while the urge to smash the person in the mouth or race out of the room is on the brink of overpowering you. You have to seem confident while your knees want to buckle and your hands tremble and sweat. You have to think and speak clearly even though your mind is full of panicked and angry voices all shouting at once or the gears in your brain seemed to have locked. You know how important it is to keep your heart open and listen, even though all you hear are your own parts complaining about how hurt or mad they are.

In such situations, most people are relieved if they are able to pretend to be in control and succeed in keeping their extreme impulses from taking over. They are happy that they don't say or do something they will later regret. Is it possible not just to pretend to feel confident, compassionate, clear, and calm but to actually be in that state even while you are highly triggered? Because many of us have been socialized to believe that we have only one personality, this idea is foreign: "You are either angry or you are calm. How can you be both at the same time?" Once you get to know your parts and your Self, you understand that it is possible. Your Self becomes the "I" in the storm—the calm center of the inner tornado of your triggered parts and the outer hurricane of upset parts in the people around you.

Achieving that state requires that you do the opposite of what you are used to doing. Ordinarily you feel the impulse to lash out and then try to control it with shame (*I'm bad for feeling angry*), scare tactics (*I'll devastate him*), or minimizing (*It's not that big a deal anyway*), all of which foster inner polarization. The angry part feels discounted, and the protectors are overburdened with responsibility for controlling the situation. If, instead, you immediately attend to the impulse with compassion and confidence, with inner words like, "I get that this is making you very upset, but I can handle it. Let me speak for you right now, and we'll talk more later about how to go from here," parts are often able to not blend with you totally so you (as your Self) can be present with your partner even while a part is fuming inside. Later, when you're alone, you can talk to the part about all of its concerns and make a plan of action or help it unburden. The goal of maintaining Self-leadership with someone who provokes you is not to get that person to change, although that is often a fortunate side effect because your Self may elicit their Self. Instead, you interact from your Self for its own sake—for the growth that comes from showing your parts that they can trust you.

SPEAKING FOR RATHER THAN FROM

The practice of speaking for, rather than from, parts when they are triggered is an important aspect of Self-leadership. When people receive a message from you, it has two components: the content (the actual words) and the energy behind the words. When your protective parts are upset and speak directly to another person, invariably they will trigger parts in the other. When, on the other hand, you listen to your protectors and then speak for them, from your Self, the message is received in a very different way, even if you use the same words that your parts are saying. Your words lose their judgmental sting or their off-putting desperation and coerciveness. Instead, your respect and compassion for the other person will be heard in addition to the courage of your convictions.

The Catholic theologian Thomas Merton translated a Taoist story, "The Empty Boat" by the Chinese philosopher Zhuangzi, that is relevant here.

If a man is crossing a river

And an empty boat collides with his skiff,

Even though he be a bad-tempered man

He will not become very angry.

But if he sees a man in the boat,

He will shout at him to steer clear.

If the shout is not heard, he will shout again,

And yet again, and begin cursing.

And all because there is somebody in the boat.

Yet if the boat were empty,

He would not be shouting, and not angry.

If you can empty your own boat

Crossing the river of the world,

No one will oppose you,

No one will seek to harm you. . . .

Such is the perfect man:

His boat is empty.[3]

Thus, by getting your parts to relax and trust you to speak for them, you become an empty vessel that can collide with other people without making them feel demeaned, competitive, pushed, repulsed, or otherwise protective. You have emptied your boat of egoistic parts, but calling it empty is misleading because your emptied vessel becomes filled with Self energy. Self energy has a soothing effect on any parts it touches, whether they are in you or in another person.

When your parts trust that you will speak for them, they feel less driven to take over and explode at people. What they really want is to have a voice—to be listened to by you and to have their position represented to others. Like people who have not been able to be authentic and fully express themselves, most parts don't need dramatic, cathartic expression—just acknowledgment and representation.

SELF-LEADERSHIP AS A WAY OF INTERACTING

These practices—remaining the "I" in the storm or the empty vessel, and speaking for rather than from your parts—can be combined into a general way of relating as a couple when you have conflict. That way includes the following steps. When you begin to fight, each of you can: (1) pause, (2) focus inside and find the parts that are triggered, (3) ask those parts to relax and let you speak for them, (4) tell your partner about what you found inside (speak for your parts), and (5) listen to your partner from your open-hearted Self.

When a couple is embattled and each focuses inside, as in step 2, usually they only hear from their protectors. If it feels safe enough, moving an extra step toward vulnerability can reap big rewards. That step involves staying inside long enough to learn about the exiles that your protectors are guarding, and then telling your partner about those basement children. In most cases, when one partner has the courage to reveal the vulnerability that drives their protectiveness, the atmosphere immediately softens and the couple shifts toward Self-to-Self communication.

Sometimes that isn't possible because either your protectors won't reveal your exiles to you or, if they do reveal them, they don't trust that it's safe for your partner to know about them. Sometimes it truly isn't safe. Your partner may have parts that automatically react to vulnerability with contempt or that may use the revelation against you in a later fight. When that is the case, I would work with each of you separately before inviting such exposure.

About a month into our therapy, Helen had told Kevin to leave, and he had found an apartment. Now Kevin wanted to return home. He said he had done several months of therapy, which he acknowledged had been difficult but helpful, and he was lonely. With uncharacteristic tenderness, he told Helen he missed her and sounded as though he meant it. Helen wasn't ready. She said she could see some changes in how he treated her, but she didn't trust that he could maintain them. She worried that he was trying now but would regress as soon as he got back and felt comfortable.

Their tone was totally different from earlier sessions. They were handling an extremely touchy subject with caring and sensitivity. I was quite moved as I witnessed this tentative peeking out from behind their castle walls and tiptoeing toward each other. Perhaps inevitably, however, Kevin's controller couldn't restrain itself and suddenly hijacked him.

Helen had just repeated that she liked this new version of him when Kevin's tone shifted abruptly. In a voice that was familiar to Helen and, by then, to me, he said angrily that he thought she liked torturing him this way—that keeping him out of the house was her way to get revenge. Helen looked as though she had been punched in the stomach. Forcefully, I told Kevin to stop talking and asked them both to focus inside to find the parts that were "up" in that moment.

There is significant danger in helping couples become more open to each other after years of pain and distance. Life isn't great while they relate from behind their castle walls, but they can't hurt each other in the way they can when they start to drop their guard. Previously insulated exiles are exposed, out in the open air, hopeful but raw. Your partner's hurtful words, which used to bounce off your castle walls, now deliver body blows to your exposed vulnerability. For this reason, unlike many couples therapists, I don't encourage couples to try to open to each other until I trust that they won't be devastated by their partner's protectors. This is why I had told Kevin and Helen not to look to each other for any closeness during the several months while I primarily worked individually with them. I waited to make that suggestion until I trusted that when, inevitably, they hurt each other, they had the ability to heal the inner damage themselves and could return to Self-leadership.

When Kevin's and Helen's eyes were closed, I told them to stay inside until they had found the protectors that were activated, as well as the parts those protectors guarded, and not to come back out until they could speak for those parts. Kevin opened his eyes after a few minutes, but Helen stayed inside silently for almost ten minutes while Kevin and I waited.

Kevin said he had found the controlling part that had hijacked him earlier, and he apologized to Helen for allowing it to take over. He said that behind it was a lonely baby that he hadn't known about before. The controller told him that it could no longer stand the long weekends alone because the baby got so desperate when he had no human contact. It began to feel increasingly worthless and panicked that it was going to die. When Helen wouldn't budge despite Kevin's respectful and loving requests to come home, the controller felt as though it had no choice—it had to take over and try the old guilt tactics that used to work because it didn't know if he could make it through another empty weekend.

Helen said she appreciated his apology and that she had often sensed that desperate baby in him. She said that when she focused inside, she was immediately bombarded by her rageful part, which was saying, "See, I told you he wasn't any different! He's still a bully! You never should have opened up, and don't ever do it again!" It took a while for her to calm that protector enough to get to the younger one that had been devastated by Kevin's eruption. When Helen first found that girl, she was frozen, as if in shock, but Helen was able to hold her and remind her of what they had worked on with me—that Helen would care for the little girl no matter what Kevin did. Helen had become the primary caretaker for her exiles. When the rageful part saw that Helen could calm the girl, it relaxed and let Helen come back to speak to Kevin for them.

Kevin said he had no idea that his controller had that impact on her because all he ever saw was her rage. This is a common problem when couples fight. Because it is their protectors that do the actual battling, neither ever sees the behind-the-scenes damage that their protectors do. It's like when the US Air Force bombs a country and we never see the videos of destroyed lives and homes. It's much harder to vote for war when you become aware of its real consequences, whether the war is between nations or individuals. That is one reason that revealing your exiles, rather than only your protectors, creates such an immediate softening. With that information, Kevin's inner defense department lost a great deal of its influence over him. He told Helen he would work with that baby so as to further disarm his controller.

That was an important statement. The temptation for the offending partner in situations like that is to promise to control their hurtful parts. Yet until Kevin could heal his baby, it's unlikely that he could stop his controller from bullying Helen, even with the knowledge of how much it hurt her. If he made that promise and then broke it, Helen would feel betrayed, thinking, *Now he knows how much it hurts me, and yet he still does it.*

This is one of the hallmarks of IFS—we don't expect a protector to change until the exile it protects has been healed so that the person is in less need of protection. This awareness bypasses so many of the binds that couples enter when they expect their partner to be able to control their protectors and are constantly disappointed when they can't.

I told Helen not to expect that Kevin's controller would be totally out of her life until he had done that work. She replied that she was less vulnerable to it now that she could comfort her parts, but she still didn't want him in the house until he was further along in his inner work. Kevin now agreed, saying that, after this discussion, he wanted to get to the point where being alone didn't bother him as much.

This is a good example of the power of parts detecting when couples are in conflict. The simple act of getting each partner to stop, listen inside, and speak for rather than from their parts turned a potential disaster into an opportunity to deepen trust and understanding between them. As Gottman found, couples will always argue in hurtful ways. The goal isn't to train them to always fight fair—it's to help them repair the damage inside themselves and to regain their Self-to-Self connection afterward. Let's talk a bit about that repair process.

REPARATIONS

John Gottman's research demonstrated that the form of the fight is less predictive of problems in a marriage than how long it takes the couple to get back on track. It seems that the key to helping a couple lies less in reducing the number or even intensity of their fights and more in improving the repair process after a fight. The problem with fights is that extreme protectors of each partner tend to terrorize the exiles of the other, adding to the pool of burdens in each person and to the perception of the other as dangerous. If, soon after the fight, each partner can enter Self-leadership, allow the other to speak about the effect of the fight on their exiles, and then deliver a heartfelt apology to those hurting parts, neither walks away with additional burdens.

In addition, if the repair happens quickly, each partner learns to trust that things can be rocky but that they can recover rapidly. This knowledge helps each of them not panic when their protectors are heading into a conflictual pattern. Often it's not the conflict itself that makes fighting so scary—it's the dread that it will lead to days or weeks of distance and mutual contempt. Once a couple has confidence that the break in their connection is quite temporary, it's much easier to hold some degree of Self-leadership even when protective parts are revved up. We will go into more detail about this repair process in a later section.

REMAINING THE "I" IN THE STORM

During the following week, Kevin's controller made several appearances but something was different. He said that he could feel the controller welling up in his gut, and a couple of times he actually tried to stop it from taking over but he couldn't. While it was hectoring Helen, though, he sensed himself, almost like an observer, thinking that it probably felt the need to distance from her because he had been vulnerable in the session. Kevin commented that it was a very strange experience to simultaneously feel the contempt of the controller and the calm of his observing Self.

Helen had a similar experience. Her rage rose immediately to meet Kevin's challenge and she felt the usual physiological surges, but she also found herself staying somewhat separate from it and talking to it inside. She said she reminded her rage that I had predicted Kevin's behavior and that it was just his controller doing its thing. In each case, after a couple of sharp exchanges, they both calmed down quickly and made a repair, during which Kevin spoke for the controller's fear about having been so exposed in the session.

For most people with delicate exiles, when a protector takes over, they become completely blended with it. An important shift takes place when you are able to maintain a kind of dual consciousness, when even if you can't stop the part, somewhere inside you know that it is a temporary hijacking—thunderclouds have rolled in but the sun will soon return.

When you can remain the "I" in the inner and outer storm in this way, the perspective you can maintain goes a long way toward short-circuiting the vicious cycles that keep couples storming for weeks, months, or even decades. You can keep the other protectors that usually jump in—hopelessness, fear of abandonment, self-loathing, or a sense of being trapped—from escalating things and instead can return quickly to Self-leadership and make a repair. Over time, you will find that you can even talk protectors down before they take over, but that only comes after your exiles are considerably less vulnerable.

In the ensuing weeks, Helen reported that Kevin's controller popped out from time to time, but during a couple of those appearances she was able to not take the bait. Instead, she forcefully reminded him that he could no longer talk to her that way, but she spoke without the usual rush of emotion. Instead, her heart remained open to him—even as she stopped him, she felt sorry for him that he was still so fragile as to rely on the controller. Kevin remembered those episodes clearly, too. He said that he was amazed to discover that when Helen stayed calm and clear, his controller was immediately deflated. Since Helen's reaction no longer fed it, it petered out. He also joked that he found Helen's ability to do that very sexy.

WHEN YOU ARE YOUR OWN PRIMARY CARETAKER

What Helen and Kevin learned is a common phenomenon with conflict in general. When extreme parts are met by Self, they lose their steam.

Consequently, when one partner stays Self-led and resists the invitation to the predictable dance, the pattern is broken. Sometimes the triggered partner will initially escalate to try to engage the other, but if that partner stays steady, the game has changed. To remind you once more, however, staying Self-led in the face of your partner's protectors is very difficult until your parts trust you as their primary caretaker. When you can give yourself at least some of what you need, as Helen was able to, your partner's outbursts appear much more like the childlike tantrums they are than as threats to your well-being. As a bonus, you become much more attractive to your partner.

The author John Welwood provides a good summary of this process: "When I no longer put what is essentially a spiritual longing on my partner, this frees her of a great burden—to make my life work, to fill up my abyss, to be the instrument of my salvation. It also frees me to see and love her as a real person, and to appreciate the real gifts she brings into my life."[4] When Kevin told Helen he would work with that baby, he began to lift the burden of caring for it from her shoulders and began to lose the "mother transference" that kept him from really seeing her.

In addition, as both partners become the primary caretakers of their own parts, they no longer need to create neo-exiles in the other person. Their former need to have their partner get rid of certain parts was driven by their exiles' insecure vulnerability and their protectors' need to recruit their partner to care for those exiles in particular ways and not others. When your exiles trust you, your partner's conduct becomes less a matter of urgent importance and more just something you can be curious about.

In a later session, Kevin was able to approach and love that baby, this time while Helen watched. He witnessed scenes of it crying desperately in a crib while no one came. He said he had heard that his mother had had postpartum depression but never thought much about it. Now he entered the scene, took the baby to his chest, and wept shamelessly. As he described this between sobs, I looked at Helen. She was crying silently. When Kevin was done retrieving the baby, Helen came close to him and told him how moved she was and how much, over the years, she had longed to see this compassionate side that she knew was in him somewhere. She also expressed deep regret that the baby had suffered so severely.

Kevin silently took in Helen's offering of love. Then, when she talked of the baby, he broke into tears again. She held him while he wailed with the transcendent force of someone who has wanted to let loose for decades. I was crying, too. It moves me deeply to watch previously hostile couples finally connect in this way.

ANTICIPATING TROUBLE

Helen held Kevin until it was almost time to stop the session. He seemed foggy and sheepish, and said he was exhausted. She said she was very happy. I told them that this session was beautiful for me to participate in and that it was important that they know this level of connection is possible. I felt compelled to warn them, however, that since they both had been so vulnerable, their protectors were likely to return with a vengeance whenever the other made the slightest false move. In fact, since they were still separated, I suggested that they minimize contact until our next session.

I'm not a person who takes pleasure in raining on people's intimacy parades, but I learned the hard way that such warnings are necessary. Even after all the work they each had done to become their own primary caretaker, a "breakthrough" session like this one was a setup. Their protectors would be on high alert, and the appearance of one from either side could trigger an escalation that would leave each of them convinced that the session had been a sham. That might happen despite my warning, but at least if it did, since I predicted it, I could tell them it was normal and help them to not overreact. Often it's not the initial protective reaction that's the problem—it's all the hopelessness and fear that rush in afterward and create enduring negative overrides. If I could help them manage their expectations, the endless protective chain reaction would be broken.

The process of couples therapy often goes that way. The partners take a few steps toward each other and then get scared, and they distance for a while. That's a natural process, and I have learned to respect it instead of trying to push couples toward consistent closeness.

I hear many complaints from one partner that the other one treats everyone else better than them. They say they can't understand this because it should be the opposite—you should treat the one you love better, not worse, than everyone else. That complaint makes sense until you realize that no one can hurt you like your partner can. As we discussed earlier, your partner is the designated redeemer of your exiles, and what they do affects those vulnerable parts of you more than any other person does. Because of this fact, it is unrealistic to expect that the two of you will be able to have perfect Self-to-Self conversations about intense issues until you both become the primary caretakers of your own exiles. Most people have many exiles, so reaching that point can be a lengthy process. In the meantime, in addition to mastering the art of the good repair and remaining the "I" in the storm, another perspective can help you weather the accordion-like rhythm of your relationship: understanding and appreciating your partner as a valuable tor-mentor.

PARTNER AS TOR-MENTOR

Generally, what your partner provokes in you is what you need to heal. If, when they hurt you, you can focus inside and go behind the protectors to the exiles they protect, you have a map that will lead you directly to a kind of buried treasure. You can use your relationship to access parts that might take years of therapy to reach—your attachment injuries—that is, the exiles that were burdened when you were young and that are looking for redemption. Healing those parts will enrich your life enormously, regardless of what happens in your relationship. And if both of you do this, your relationship becomes a container for tremendous intimacy. You can come home to each other's Self.

Thus, the constant and futile attempts to force your partner to change lead to despair. When you can step out of the automatic dances long enough to use the map to buried treasure that your relationship affords, you have hope. You learn that you don't need your partner to heal or complete you. And as you heal, it's not uncommon to discover that things in your relationship that once seemed like huge boulders in your path to intimacy magically shrink into pebbles.

But the concept of partner-as-valuable-tor-mentor is a hard sell for most of us. Our protective managers are organized to make the external world less threatening and to keep us away from our internal world. Inside us lie the emotions they are trying to stay away from. Why would they want to go in there? Most people who come to me for couples therapy are focused exclusively on getting their partner to change. They have little awareness of the damage their own cannonballs do and tremendous awareness of their partner's destructive capacity. It is natural for their parts to want to eliminate the external threat rather than look inward. It's always difficult to get each person to go inside toward their own pain rather than attack the perceived source of it in their partner. Why should we go to the dungeon when the castle is under siege?

Most people dance the same dances, even with different partners, because they never bother to look inside. They spend their lives striving for redemption they don't need and being disappointed in each chosen redeemer whom they try to change to fit the bill. Once people go inside and unburden these parts, they are released from this self-perpetuating curse.

Actually, we can use any difficulty in life that produces an extreme reaction as a path to parts we need to heal. As the Buddhist nun Pema Chödrön writes, "Other people trigger the karma we haven't worked out. They mirror us and give us the chance to befriend all of that ancient stuff that we carry around like a backpack full of boulders." She adds, "The idea of karma is that you continually get the teachings you need in order to open your heart. To the degree that you didn't understand in the past how to stop protecting your soft spot, how to stop armoring your heart, you are given this gift of teachings in the form of your life, to give you everything you need to learn how to open further."[5] Chödrön relates the story of the great Indian Buddhist teacher Atisha, who was going to Tibet. Atisha knew he had unconscious blind spots that he could only find by being provoked. He was concerned because he had heard that the people of Tibet were good-natured, flexible, and open—not irritating enough to push his buttons. So he brought along his mean-spirited, indulgent Bengali tea boy, whom he knew would help him get where he needed to go. There is a similar story about the philosopher G. I. Gurdjieff. In a spiritual community he led was an old, belligerent, selfish man who upset everyone. When the man threatened to leave, Gurdjieff paid him to stay. The rest of the group was incensed that this obnoxious man was being paid to be there, while they had to pay. Gurdjieff said, "This man is like yeast for bread. Without him here you would never really learn about anger, irritability, patience, and compassion. That is why you pay me, and why I hire him."[6]

We can understand the obnoxious parts of our partner as our Bengali tea boys or our obnoxious old men—as what might be called our tor-mentors. They mentor us by tormenting us. That is, our partner often leads us to a mother lode of gold because of the unconscious reasons we selected them. As children, most of us were given sizable burdens by at least one parent or caretaker. Whether we felt abandoned, shamed, betrayed, neglected, coerced, ignored, manipulated, smothered, or terrorized, those experiences left us feeling like a worthless object or one that is highly valued but only as something to make our parents feel good. Many of us felt invisible—as if no one saw our Self and instead only saw what they wanted us to be or mixed us up with something inside themselves they hated. When our partner does anything resembling what happened earlier, it triggers the parts of us that are stuck back in those days, which are key exiles. As aggravating as our partners can be, they are invaluable guides pointing down the royal road to healing. They are the best guides, much better than angry old men or tea boys.

This partner-as-tor-mentor concept contradicts many prevalent beliefs about intimate relationships. For example, most of us believe that if our relationship involves frequent struggle, we must be with the wrong person. Committed partnerships should be full of loving moments because we should have found our perfectly compatible soul mate. Our partner should heal us and make us whole, not antagonize or constrain us.

What most of my clients find is that even when their partner is perfectly loving, it triggers parts of them that don't trust they are lovable, that the love will last, or that someone who loves them deserves their love.

Because of our burdens and our reasons for choosing a partner, we will be triggered in important ways by that person. The question is whether we will use the relationship to illuminate dark dungeons we need to clear out or avoid looking in those dungeons by focusing instead on the partner.

VIRTUOUS CYCLES

I continued to work with the Bradys in couples sessions for several months. Eventually Helen asked Kevin to come home. I was impressed with Kevin when he responded with uncharacteristic sensitivity. He asked her with sincerity if she was sure. He said he had learned to be alone without panicking, so he didn't want her to feel any pressure. Helen said she could tell that was true and that his newfound ability to soothe himself made her enjoy being with him more than she ever had before. Their transition back to living together wasn't totally seamless, but they both felt confident in their ability to handle the rough spots.

Once couples can maintain a certain level of Self-to-Self connectedness, they begin to reverse the vicious cycles and start virtuous ones. Not only do they begin accepting, rather than rejecting, each other's bids for affection, but they also achieve what might be called "positive override." Gradually the swing-vote parts in each person's inner family, described earlier, begin to move back from the anti-partner group to the pro group. Whereas you saw their thoughtless or hurtful behaviors as cruel while your anti group was large and dominant, now the same behaviors become tolerable quirks when seen through the loving eyes of the pro majority. Whereas before, you never gave your partner a break, now they have lots of leeway, and you can again see the qualities that attracted you to them originally.

As you sense that you are no longer walking on eggshells, your protectors relax more, releasing more of your Self, so you increasingly sense Self-to-Self connection with your partner, otherwise known as love. With that love as a foundation, the sun doesn't totally disappear anymore when the storm clouds roll in, so you no longer overreact to the dark periods in your relationship.

Finally, because both you and your partner are becoming the primary caretakers of your own exiles, the protectors in each of you drop their partner-changing projects. When this happens, your neo-exiles begin to sense a new acceptance from your partner and start to believe that she might allow room for them in your life. They stop sabotaging, and they also leave the ranks of the anti group. The virtuous cycle spirals upward.

The later sessions with Kevin and Helen were easy. Kevin's focus of frustration had shifted. Whereas before, he would complain that he never had enough time to do his job adequately, now he wished that it weren't so consuming. With the achievement monkey off his back, he was able to enjoy time with Helen and the kids without the constant nagging from his striving critic. Kevin didn't quit his job, but he did begin writing less and spending more time with his family. Helen noticed that his old carping had abated at home and he was more available to her—for example, talking to her in the car instead of turning on the radio to distract himself. At a party, a physician at Kevin's hospital told Helen that colleagues had noticed how much he had lightened up. His residents no longer felt terrified to speak to him. Physically, both she and I could see a difference. His face was softer and his posture less rigid.

Helen had also changed. During the separation, she had reached out to a small group of women friends who had been tremendously supportive throughout. While they had advised her not to let Kevin come back, they hadn't seen the changes in him that she had. Even after Kevin returned home, Helen continued to meet with them regularly, which initially triggered Kevin's controller. But he was able to catch it himself and apologize.

She said that since marrying Kevin, she'd neglected the parts of her that loved to play with friends because he had wanted her home with him, even though he was usually in his study writing. She said she would never do that again and was glad that Kevin could now support her independence. Helen was liberating her neo-exiles, and Kevin was making room for them in their shared life. Kevin had found courageous love.

When both you and your partner commit to this Self-led way of relating, it doesn't ensure that your relationship will be forever harmonious. It does, however, mean that you both will use it to learn about and heal the burdens you brought to it. When you do that, you are doing what you are here to do, and your relationship will benefit. Your protective parts can relax with the knowledge that even if you have a big fight, your partner will do their work and will then show up again as their Self. Each of you will use the fight to clear more obstacles to your Self-to-Self relating. That knowledge brings the hope of connectedness, which helps couples persevere through the dark nights in their relationships.

On the other hand, when you are the only one consistently doing this work and your partner isn't, parts of you will be frustrated, and you may ultimately decide to leave the relationship. You may feel as though you have learned what there was to learn with that partner and it's time to move on. In the meantime, however, the Self-leadership way of interacting is still a valuable practice, regardless of what the other person does. It is a more difficult practice because your parts will be saying, "We have to take over because their parts have," but when you can remain Self-led in the face of extreme parts of the other person, your Self earns tremendous respect from your parts. This brings new meaning to the term Self-confidence.

Next, I will be more concrete about the steps involved in using your relationship to learn and heal—in letting your partner be your tor-mentor who evokes key trailheads in you.

CHAPTER FIVE

Getting Practical: How to Bring In Courageous Love

I am trying to learn that this playful man who teases me is the same as that serious man talking money to me so seriously he does not even see me anymore and that patient man offering me advice in times of trouble and that angry man slamming the door as he leaves the house. I have often wanted the playful man to be more serious, and the serious man to be less serious, and the patient man to be more playful. As for the angry man, he is a stranger to me and I do not feel it is wrong to hate him. Now I am learning that if I say bitter words to the angry man as he leaves the house, I am at the same time wounding the others, the ones I do not want to wound—the playful man teasing, the serious man talking money, and the patient man offering advice. Yet I look at the patient man, for instance, whom I would want above all to protect from such bitter words as mine, and though I tell myself he is the same man as the others, I can only believe I said those words not to him but to another, my enemy, who deserved all my anger.[1]

With those words, the fiction writer Lydia Davis may capture well your dilemma at this point in the book. Maybe you are starting to understand the benefit of this multiplicity perspective and the impact of your anger on your partner's vulnerable parts, but you still don't know how to handle their protectors. How do you put this philosophy into action?

This is the how-to chapter where I present specific steps for couples to transform the problems explored in the preceding chapters. We begin with finding and healing the parts that drive the protective patterns in your relationship. Next, you will learn how to have Self-led conversations during conflict, how to repair any damage that occurs, and finally how to create lasting intimacy.

FOLLOWING THE RELATIONSHIP TRAILHEAD

Look again at the list of manifestations of protective parts on pages 89–90 and pick one of those or something else in you that your partner triggers. Once you identify one of these thoughts, emotions, or behaviors, focus on it until you can find the source of it in or around your body. Then notice how you feel toward the protective part that was making you think, feel, or act that way. Ask any other parts that are making you dislike or fear the targeted protector to relax and step back (to separate from you) so you can get to know the target part. Continue to do that until you feel curious about the target part and then ask it what it wants you to know about itself. Don't try to think about what it would say—just wait with your focus on it until some kind of impression or answer comes to you.

To simplify this process, you can just ask yourself the following questions:

What am I thinking or feeling about my partner?

Where in or around my body do I find those thoughts or feelings?

How do I feel toward the part that's causing me to have those thoughts or feelings?

Are other parts willing to let me be curious about this part?

What does the part want me to know about itself?

What is it afraid would happen if it didn't do this job?

When you ask a protector what it wants you to know, initially it may continue to rant about your partner or about you. Be patient with it and continue to ask what it's afraid would happen if it didn't say or do those things, or why those things bother it so much. At some point, the protector will begin to tell you more about why it's so upset, and you will likely learn about how: (1) it feels exiled by your partner, (2) it protects a part that has been hurt before your partner entered the scene or a part that feels exiled by your partner, or (3) it is polarized with another part of you that it is afraid will take over and dominate your relationship. Below I'll elaborate on each of these three possibilities and how to handle them.

WHEN A PART FEELS EXILED BY THE RELATIONSHIP

If the part tells you that it feels shamed by or unacceptable to your partner, first get to know what your partner does that makes the neo-exile feel that way, and find out whether it is stuck in the past at a time when it felt similarly exiled in an earlier relationship. You can also find out what the part would prefer to do if it were fully accepted by you and your partner. This may be quite different from its initial desires because, just like children who feel like outcasts in a family, when parts feel shut out, they become extreme and make inner demands that often don't reflect their deepest desires. The voice that was constantly lobbying for you to have an affair, for example, may turn out to be a lively, fun-loving part of you that your partner constantly calls immature and shames you out of. Once you listen to how the part has felt abandoned by you, it can let you know that it only wanted an affair because it didn't have a place in your life anymore and that if you could find room for it somehow, even if not in your relationship, it would be quite content.

After hearing all this from your part, you can discuss with your partner what you learned. It is important, however, that your partner has asked their parts to relax and allow them to listen from their Self so that they will hear what you say without distortion and with curiosity and compassion.

For example, Claire, an outgoing extrovert, felt trapped in her relationship with Gil, a more private person who wanted to limit their friendships to a small number of people, mostly family. Claire contended that she could live with their differences around socializing if Gil let her go out on her own with friends. Gil said that because they both worked long hours, there was little time for them to be together, so if Claire went out as much as she wanted, he'd hardly see her.

In the early days of their relationship, they fought long and hard over this issue, and Claire went out frequently despite Gil's protests. After their daughter was born, Claire no longer had the energy to party nor to battle with Gil. Claire acceded to the lifestyle that was comfortable for Gil, focusing instead on balancing motherhood and her career. Now, with her daughter in her teens, Claire was ready to renew her neglected friendships, and Gil was feeling abandoned. Their conflicts had taken an ugly turn recently when Claire told Gil she was bored with him and couldn't stand his possessiveness. Gil replied that if he wasn't enough for her, she should find someone else.

I asked each of them to focus inside on the feelings generated by their recent fight. Claire saw an image of herself as a teenager enclosed in a jail, banging on the bars to be released. That part told her it had always felt Gil's disapproval and never wanted her to marry him. Not only did he dissuade her from going out, but on the rare occasions when they did go to parties together, he gave her critical looks whenever she started having fun. When Claire asked the girl why Gil's disapproval bothered her so much, she immediately saw scenes from hurtful fights with her father over curfew violations and drinking. Claire had been the rebel in her uptight family, and this nonconformist adolescent part of her carried intense feelings of unworthiness and shame.

Gil also found a teenager, a boy who was lonely and felt like a loser in junior high school. The boy was too shy to have girlfriends, and he couldn't keep up with the caustic repartee of his male peers, so he had retreated into his studies. That strategy paid off in adulthood since his prominence in his academic career is what originally attracted Claire, who was a former student. Claire's suggestions that Gil was boring triggered all the loser feelings the boy carried, which Gil described as the worst feelings he had ever experienced. Gil's boy was very attracted to Claire's liveliness because if she liked him, it proved that he wasn't so boring. When she was with others, however, the boy was sure she'd find someone better and leave him.

Simply disclosing to each other what they learned from their parts went a long way toward defusing their battles. Gil knew Claire's father and said he could understand why she would have rebelled. He said he didn't want to be in that father-like role anymore and was committed to helping his inner boy with his shame so that her teenager could feel at home in their relationship. Claire said she felt glad that Gil revealed that boy part because he seemed so assured and together most of the time that she had thought he was just a control freak. She had no idea that her complaints had such a hurtful impact. She agreed to help her teenage part unload the feelings it carried from wrestling with her father so that it didn't overreact to Gil's need for closeness.

WHEN A PART IS PROTECTING HURT OR EXILED PARTS

Ask your protector what it's afraid would happen if it didn't do what it does. If, in response, it says that your partner would hurt you, ask if it would allow you to get to know and maybe help the part it protects that would be hurt. If it gives its permission, focus on the hurt part and ask it not to overwhelm you as you listen to it. If it agrees not to overwhelm, ask what it wants you to know. If it shows you recent slights from your partner, witness those with compassion but also ask if those are related to any events further in the past. You may then see scenes of attachment reinjuries—times in your relationship when your partner betrayed you or was unavailable when you were vulnerable. After fully witnessing how painful those episodes were, ask the part if those events relate to anything else in the past. You may find yourself revisiting similarly wounding events from your childhood.

Once you have let the child in those scenes know that you understand how hurtful those events were, you can return to your partner and share what you learned. It is important, however, that your partner is prepared to be Self-led during this sharing; otherwise, it is easy for your hurt exiles to feel reinjured by your partner's response. If it feels safe and your partner's Self is available, tell them what you learned about your protector and what it protects.

There are multiple examples of this dynamic scattered throughout this book because it is the most common one. For an in-depth illustration, return to the work with Kevin and Helen Brady in the previous chapter.

WHEN A PART IS POLARIZED WITH ANOTHER PART

In response to your inquiries, the protector may let you know that it's afraid if it stops what it's doing, another part will take over. If this is the case, ask if it's willing to let you get to know the part it's afraid of in order to see if that one is indeed likely to take over and if it is as bad as this part thinks. If it agrees, focus on the other part and see what it wants you to know about itself.

You may learn that this part is extreme because it's reacting to the dominance of the original part. If that dominant one would lighten up, this part wouldn't need to continue to act in such an extreme manner. At some point, you may be able to bring the two polarized parts together to interact directly with each other while you play the role of their therapist, ensuring that they communicate respectfully to each other.

For example, Alex's chronic anxiety drove Maya crazy. He was constantly afraid when she left the house or when he had to make a presentation at his job. Of course, her irritation with his dependence only made him more insecure and certain that she would leave him. I had them both focus on the parts involved in this pattern. When Alex listened to his anxious part, it said it was afraid that if it let him feel okay, his macho part would take over again. Alex then told me that earlier in their marriage, he had been the complete opposite—hard-drinking, competitive, and overbearing. After going to rehab for alcoholism, he stopped drinking and became anxious. The anxious part said that when it kept him dependent, he treated Maya much better, his life was in control, and he was no longer ruining his health. It wasn't about to let up unless we could prove to it that the macho guy wouldn't return with a vengeance. When Alex listened to the macho guy part, it said, "I hate the weakness of the anxious part;

it makes me act like a sissy. I take over to make you a real man and not a dependent wimp." I helped Alex bring the two polarized parts together in his mind to discuss their issues with each other, with Alex moderating their conversation. As they faced each other and interacted directly, each could see that the other wasn't as bad as it had previously believed. This realization launched a depolarizing process within Alex that ultimately included working with the exiles that both parts protected.

Not surprisingly, Maya had become polarized with each of Alex's extreme protectors. Maya shared with Alex's anxious part a tremendous investment in not letting his macho guy return to power and became enraged at any sign of its presence, but she was also fed up with his sniveling and anxiety. She found a frustrated part of her that had a great deal of impatience with, and contempt for, Alex's clinginess. There was also a rageful protector that carried the accumulated resentment of years living under the domination of Alex's alcoholic, macho part.

Thus, if you have an internal polarization, the parts on each side may become so extreme that they also become polarized with parts in your partner such that an internal polarization creates a similar external polarization. In turn, as your partner fights to eliminate your parts, they become increasingly entrenched and polarized with your other parts, as well as with your partner, and so on. Because it is the nature of polarization to escalate over time, small ones, if unaddressed, can grow to the point of blotting out the love in a relationship and can keep each partner's internal system in turmoil.

REVEALING YOUR PARTS

In many of the examples so far in this book, when the person focused inside, they not only learned about a protector but also about the exile it protected. Telling a partner about the protector was helpful, but it was only when the person revealed the exile behind it that things really softened. Let me issue a few caveats here. First, when you focus inside, don't be surprised if you only hear from your protector and aren't able to get a sense of the part it protects. This is common, especially at first, and only means that the protector doesn't feel it is safe for you to know about that vulnerability. It may be that the part doesn't think you can handle that information, or it may so fear your partner that it's not going to let you be vulnerable while they're around. That's okay. Just telling your partner about your protectors will start a process that can make things safer down the road for you to discover your exiles.

Second, if you do learn about your exiles, it may not be safe to disclose them to your partner, so don't feel any pressure to do so until you trust that they can give a Self-led response. On the other hand, when you do learn about the exiles your partner triggers and feel safe enough to tell your partner about them—and then feel heard by your partner—you've broken the deathless cycle of cold and hot wars between your protectors and have begun a journey toward intimacy.

Third, I have tried to write this book in such a way that you and your partner can try to do this work without the help of a professional. For some of you, this will work. Many readers, however, will find that they can do pieces of it on their own but need the presence of a therapist for other pieces. The Self-led practice described above of listening inside and disclosing what you find to your partner will go a long way toward each of you becoming the primary caretaker of your parts so your partner can be their secondary caretaker. But it won't do the whole job because your parts also need to unburden the extreme beliefs and emotions they accumulated from the past before they will fully trust you and not overreact to your partner. While some people can unburden without the help of a therapist, most cannot. Also, it's very difficult for some couples to get their protectors to stop complaining about and trying to change the other person without a third party in the room that they both trust. You can find a growing number of resources, including a practitioner directory, books, and courses available on the IFS website at ifs-institute.com.

SELF-TO-SELF DISCUSSIONS

Releasing Creative Solutions

In addition to speaking for, rather than from, your parts to your partner, you will want to discuss the issues between you in a productive way. My experience is that when couples can communicate Self to Self, creative solutions often come to them that had been unavailable when their parts were locking horns. Of course, not all issues have solutions, but Self-led conversations can help each partner at least feel understood and accepted by the other, despite continued differences.

Pre-conversation Inner Pep Talks

Given all the obstacles to Self-led communication that we have already discussed, especially around charged issues, it behooves each partner to have internal discussions with their respective protectors in advance of a conversation about relationship issues.

In such a pre-conversation inner process, you can separate from those protectors and remind them who your partner really is and what your goals really are. Protectors can become so caught up with the wrongs your partner has committed that they lose all perspective about the big picture of what's best for you or your relationship. Protectors also tend to elicit in your partner exactly the opposite of what they really want. So it is good practice for you to work with them before and during important discussions. When you do, questions like these can help:

> What are my protectors saying about this situation?
>
> What do I want the outcome of the discussion to be, and are those parts likely to get us there?
>
> If I could behave in the discussion just the way I thought would best achieve that outcome, regardless of what my partner does, what would that look like?

Are my protectors willing to trust me to handle the discussion? If not, what are they afraid would happen if they did?

Can I remember that my partner has extreme protectors that don't represent all of them and that behind them are vulnerability and love for me?

How can I help my partner trust that it is safe to not lead with their protectors?

If they do lead with their protectors, what do mine need so they don't take over in response to theirs?

If your protectors respond well to this preliminary pep talk, you will sense a difference in your body and mind. As you approach the discussion with your partner, you feel a degree of calmness inside and a curiosity about their perspective. Your heart is open, so you are able to hold your love for them despite your differences. You aren't afraid to assert your position and to speak for your parts, but you also aren't attached to a certain outcome. You know that you will be able to comfort your parts no matter how the discussion goes, so you don't come to it with a great deal of fear.

Spacious Conversations

An inner spaciousness exists when our exiles feel cared for by us. They aren't so focused on what our partner has done to hurt or neglect them, and, as a result, our protectors aren't poised for battle. When both you and your partner are in this spacious state, even major issues shrink in importance when they encounter the pleasure of your connectedness. You feel free to speak for all of your parts, so none of them feel exiled. You are able to listen to your partner without distortion or defensiveness and, consequently, they feel heard.

This is a far cry from the state that most of us are in when we begin tough discussions with our partners. It may take considerable time and effort to get your parts to relax their grip before a talk, and many protectors don't want to wait. Instead, they want to rush right in to confront your partner and get it over with. The preparation is worth the trouble, though, because the alternative—part-to-part combat—generally makes things worse. You both walk away feeling more like failures and more hopeless about your relationship, all of which makes it harder to get your parts to calm down the next time you try to talk.

Suppose you are able to enter a difficult discussion in this spacious state of Self-leadership. If you are like most people, it won't take long before you lose it and a part of you jumps up. It may not take over to the degree that you say aloud the extreme things it is saying inside, but it will taint your perspective on your partner and on the issues between you, or harden slightly your tone of voice and the content of your words. Because of this extra, biased voice in your head, you no longer really hear your partner and instead formulate your defense while they are talking. These subtle and often unconscious shifts from spaciousness to closed-mindedness and from compassion to coolness can spark escalations. Therefore, it is important to catch your parts early when they are evoked and help them trust that they can let you stay open and spacious. To do that, you have to notice what's happening in your body and your mind while you interact with your partner—a dual focus that is challenging in most situations but particularly so when your protectors want you to focus exclusively on the threat they feel your partner presents.

Parts and Self Detecting During Conflict

When I first start to work with many embattled couples, I have to stop their dialogues every few minutes and ask them to focus inside on the parts that are popping up. They often protest that they were just trying to make a point and don't understand what they were doing wrong. This stems from two problems. First, most people, when they are triggered, have no idea how they are coming across. They can describe in detail the hurtful acts of their partner but are unable to take in the impact of their own behavior when it becomes extreme. Second, most people don't know that this spacious, Self-led approach is possible, and they are highly identified with the parts that typically handle conflict for them.

If, however, I am able to get them to focus inside, they can usually find the part that was talking and will find that it is indeed trying to protect them. I mention these couples to underscore the difficulty of what I am suggesting you try to do on your own when you enter conflict. For some people, coming to realize that their protectors are not their Self is like discovering that what they thought all their life was their hair is really a wig. Many of us are so identified with certain protectors that we can't tell when they have taken over. For example, when my ex-wife, Nancy, would say something critical of me, I would defend myself in a calm, logical way that, to me, seemed to be coming from my Self. I was always confused when she would get more upset in response until I learned to check my body to see if I really was being Self-led. I found that despite seeming open and nondefensive, my heart was closed to her. Now, during intense discussions with people, I check my heart from time to time to be sure that subtle protector isn't doing the talking for me. It has a way of conveying a lack of caring for the other person that makes things worse.

So one way to detect when a part is protecting is to check your body. Most protectors have a certain predictable presence in your body that is easily discernable once you learn to notice it. There are some fearful parts of me that immediately make my forehead feel tense and pressured when I begin to argue with someone. My voice gets hard-edged and cold when another part comes in. It helps to discover your most dominant protectors, get to know their physiological impacts on you, and practice reading your body to determine how present they are. Then, during charged discussions, you can occasionally check those places in your body to discern how much those protectors are influencing you. Take another look at the list on pages 89–90 if you need reminders of common protectors.

You can also check your mind for protectors. When I'm trying to work out an issue with someone, I do my best to monitor how attached I am to winning the argument or getting them to see my point of view. I'll listen inside for any voices that are saying extreme things about the other person or are formulating a new defense or attack. On a good day, I can notice all that behind-the-scenes activity and clear it out quickly with some inner reassurance.

Yet despite having practiced this process for two decades, at times my protectors still hijack me. The couples therapist Terrence Real aptly calls it "whoosh": "Whoosh is the visceral wave, the conditioned reflex, that washes over us instantaneously. For some it is fear, for others shame, and for others still, anger. I grew up in a raging household. Whenever someone sticks something in my face, my reflexive response is a desire to knock their teeth in."[2] That kind of automatic whoosh can be very hard to stop.

There are certain people for whom it helps a great deal to have a trusted third party present when you try to work on your relationship. That third person's main job is to be the parts detector that neither of you is able to be on your own. The point here is that you won't always be able to detect your parts and stay Self-led with your partner, which is why you might want access to a therapist who can detect your parts when you can't. On the other hand, you probably can do a lot more of your own parts detecting than you think.

Self Detecting

If you have trouble detecting certain parts, it is possible instead to focus on how much your Self is embodied. As you interact with your partner, you can check frequently to see how spacious, curious, openhearted, calm, and clear you feel. Different people have different physiological cues they check to aid in their Self detecting. For some, it's their breathing; others focus on their voice. I keep noticing the state of my heart, and I also can feel a warm, vibrating energy running through my body when I am Self-led. While in that state, I speak effortlessly with no inner rehearsing. I feel connected to my partner even when we are hard at it, and I'm really interested in what is going on for her.

So as we struggle with our issues, I am simultaneously trying to engage with her while also noticing how present I am while we are interacting. Once I notice that I'm not very embodied, I know that my parts have hijacked me and that continuing to talk is not likely to be productive.

Handling a "Parts Attack"

Detecting the existence of a protector or the absence of Self is a crucial step, but it's only the first step. There are situations in which, upon noticing a part, I can use inner words to quickly reassure it and help it relax. If there were a microphone in my head at such a moment, you might hear phrases like *Trust me*; *Remember, things always go better when you let me stay*; *I can handle this*. When that reassurance works, I feel an immediate shift toward less concern for winning the argument and greater ability to stay connected while we disagree. Sometimes I can do this without pausing the conversation, and my partner doesn't know I'm doing it. When that's not possible, I'll ask that we pause for a moment so I can calm my parts, and when I return I'll speak for those parts by giving a brief report of who was there and why.

When that doesn't work, I'll abort the conversation and suggest we break until I am better able to stay Self-led. This is often quite difficult because the whoosh protectors have me so hyped up physiologically that I can't even separate enough to know that we should take a break. Also, my more rational, lawyerly protectors are convinced that if I give them a little more time, they can get from my partner the understanding, apology, or promise of change that they think I need. They tell me it's just around the corner and that if they are allowed to present my case one more time or more forcefully or with more detail, they'll get her to give me what I deserve.

The times when you are able to separate and speak from a Self-led place despite the incredible drive to remain blended with a protector become key moments of growth in your relationship. Terrence Real agrees with the pivotal importance of "those moments when every muscle and nerve in your body is pulling you toward your old set of responses, and yet a new force lifts you up off the accustomed track toward deliberate, constructive action—toward repair."[3]

The righteousness of my protectors can still seduce me at times, and I am a person who has spent decades working with my parts. No wonder people who are unaware they even have parts, allow these parts to hijack them. They have no awareness that there is an alternative to parts wars—that Self-to-Self relating is possible and helpful. Those people may even learn communication skills and practice them when they work on issues, but often their protectors will still be doing the talking and will feel even more righteous because now they are following the rules of fair fighting. I have learned, however, that it is usually far better to stop interacting once a part hijacks and refuses to step back. I will ask my partner for a recess and suggest another time down the road to resume. I will also make it clear to her that I'll use the intervening time to work with my parts so that when we resume, I'll be better able to stay present. During that interval, I'll work by myself with my protector and what it protects, or if I can't get far on my own, I will call a therapist to help me. In this way, I take advantage of my partner's ability to be my tor-mentor—to bring up parts I need to heal—and I also do what's necessary to be more Self-led when we talk again.

You may have noticed that I didn't say I would call for a recess when I saw that my partner had been hijacked by a part. The goal is not to talk only when my partner is Self-led. This is because I believe that it is my responsibility to try to hold Self-leadership even when my partner has lost it. If I can do that, often my partner's Self returns, and my parts gain confidence in my leadership because I showed them that I could handle my partner's toughest fighters.

This speaks to the larger goals of dealing with your partner on difficult issues. I have come to see the real value of that process not as the resolution of the issues, although sometimes that happens; and when it does, it's icing on the cake. Instead, such challenging discussions are (1) opportunities to demonstrate to my parts that they can trust me even in the face of serious threat and (2) ways to access, and later heal, key exiles. If my partner holds this same perspective, our conflicts become arenas for tremendous growth, both personally and for our relationship. But if my partner doesn't see things in this way or doesn't do her inner work, I can still gain a great deal from the process.

This perspective takes you out of the position of monitoring your partner's parts and pointing them out to them. While in a conflict, trying to be your partner's parts detector is a good way to fan the flames. When people are upset, most don't appreciate being told what they are doing wrong, and it's unlikely that you will be Self-led when you identify that their part has taken over. Consequently, when I'm working with a couple, I institute the rule that they can talk about their own parts but not their partner's. So, rather than complaining, "I see that your tantrumming part is here again," you can simply say, "An angry part of me is triggered by what you're doing right now, so let's talk later."

One problem with not stopping, and instead continuing, a parts war is that when your protectors are upset, they often say hurtful or extreme things that you don't mean. As discussed earlier, they also use Gottman's Four Horsemen with impunity. If you continue, you wind up wounding your partner's exiles and creating attachment reinjuries, which further fuel their protectors. In that scenario, each fight, rather than being a chance for increasing trust in Self-leadership and personal healing, further burdens each partner's exiles with worthlessness and their protectors with distrust.

Seeing the Exiles Behind the Protectors

When your partner's protectors have totally hijacked them, and they are ranting about your faults and saying things that seem to you to be exaggerations or even fabrications, it is hard not to respond to that energy and content. I used to always take the bait when someone would say something inaccurate about what I had done, and I would respond to correct the content rather than address the hurt feeling that was driving the outburst. I have a part that felt it had to make sure all the facts were correct, as if there were some permanent record of my life somewhere that would be tarnished if I didn't constantly clarify distortions.

Now, in such situations, I can usually catch that part and quickly remind it that there is no permanent record and that I don't have to respond to either the distortions in content or the angry energy. When that protector and other ones allow my Self to stay present, I can hear and see the pain or fear behind the hurtful presentation and can respond to it with compassion. I also can listen for the truths embedded in the exaggerations—the things that I did do and can apologize for sincerely. Again, Terrence Real describes this well as he faces a tirade from his wife: "Her accusations struck me as exaggerated, distorted, and delivered from a one-up, unloving place. But, like jewels in a trash heap, there were points in her speech that were true. By sheer force of discipline, these were the only points I chose to respond to. I had strained through the 85 percent of her diatribe that seemed like nonsense, and given back the 15 percent that I could admit to."[4]

Even when you can't find any jewels in the trash heap—when it seems as if your partner is delusional—if you remain Self-led and respond to their pain rather than to their words, things improve because what they really want is for their exiles to be witnessed by you—to trust that you understand that you hurt them and regret having done that. Unfortunately, most people's protectors elicit the opposite of what they really want. Your job is to see through their walls and cannonballs to the wounded and terrified childlike exiles they heroically try to protect.

The Self-Led Repair

This brings up the topic of apologies. From personal and professional observation, I have concluded that most people aren't very good at giving clean and heartfelt apologies. If we live in a litigious and competitive culture, we are further discouraged from acknowledging hurtful mistakes. Patriarchy equates apologizing with submitting or losing. Protective parts that fear being dominated by your partner will try to convince you that conceding one point will open the door to total subjugation. Or they fear the wrath of your inner critics if you admit to yourself that you hurt your partner or aren't perfect.

So your protectors continue to defend, minimize, or even deny, both within you and to your partner. If they allow an apology, it's from a placating "Maybe this will get them to shut up" place or a groveling "I'm so bad—how can you ever forgive me?" place. At the same time, internally they either will reassure you that you didn't really do anything so bad or will make you feel totally worthless. Other common parts may also interfere with a reparative apology, but you get the picture.

When you apologize from a protector, often your partner will sense the insincerity or extremeness and will not feel witnessed. When one partner says, "Why do we have to go over that again? I've apologized many times for what I did," it is often because the other partner never received a clean apology—one uncontaminated by the discounting energy of protectors. Protector-led apologies often include qualifying phrases like "I'm sorry if I hurt you" or "I'm sorry that your feelings were hurt" and are quickly followed by a defensive explanation of why you committed the offending act or how your intentions were good and were misinterpreted. Also, because your protectors want to get it over with quickly, they often will cut off your partner's description of what you did before their exiles feel fully understood by you. As a result, they'll bring it up again—and in a more extreme way—until they feel fully witnessed. It is also common for the offending partner to issue a terse apology followed quickly by an attempt to get the partner to listen to how they were hurt at another time. "I'm sorry, but what about what you did?" Finally, there are scared, placating protectors that will exaggerate your remorse and self-deprecation to get your partner off your back. "I can't believe I did that to you. I'm such a horrible person. How can you ever forgive me?"

When, in contrast, you can calm your protectors' frenzy in your head so you are able to hear the pain beneath your partner's extremes and can hold your heart open to that pain, you will be moved to find the right words. Actually, the words matter much less than your energy. Your Self will find a way to convey how sorry you are that your partner is suffering.

What your partner wants is the same thing that exiles in general want. It involves three steps—for you to:

1. compassionately witness what happened from their perspective and appreciate how much they were hurt;
2. sincerely express your empathy for that pain and regret for your role in creating it (no matter how inadvertent); and
3. describe the steps you will take to prevent it from happening again.

Not all people need all those steps. Many feel better after receiving step 1, or 1 and 2, and don't need step 3. Step 3 is important with particularly harmful or chronic behaviors.

But there are often problems with step 3. Many hurtful behaviors are difficult to change without finding and healing the parts that drive them. Many couples find themselves in states of despair and resignation because they each have repeatedly promised the other that they would stop their hurtful behaviors and were sincere each time, only to find that over and over, they broke their promise. As long as your exiles are in highly vulnerable and neglected states, your protectors will react automatically and will repeat their harmful actions. There is only so much that willpower, self-vigilance, and good intentions can accomplish.

In many cases, then, the most realistic promise you can make in step 3 is that you will try to find and work with the parts that are behind the hurtful behavior. In the moment, this may not be as satisfying to your partner's exiles as something like "I swear I will never do that again," but you'd be surprised at how healing a statement like this can be: "I can see how often I hurt you by being so critical, so I am going to work with that critic to help it stop. It might take a while, but I'm determined to do it because I love you and don't want to keep hurting you." It gives your partner hope because they know that, perhaps with help, it is something you can actually do. For you, it continues the sacred process of using your relationship to help you find and unburden parts that keep your heart closed. When you see it that way, apologizing and committing to change no longer feel submissive. They become active and brave steps on the path to personal and relational growth—elements of courageous love.

After receiving a Self-led apology, many of the victimized partners I work with react with relief and spontaneously say they are aware that while their hurt was real, they did overreact to it and are sorry about that. They also commit to finding and working with the parts involved. In this way, ruptures of connection in your relationship, if repaired well, become rich sources of trailheads for you and your partner. Once again, your partner serves as your valued tor-mentor.

For serious breaches of trust or safety, however, the one-time genuine apology will not do the job. The offending partner needs to earn back the victim's trust over time. Again, protectors will make this difficult because after they allow you to apologize, they will encourage you not to mention the incident again ("Why touch that open wound?"), and when it does come up, they will say, "I apologized already." They will also want you to minimize or excuse your role and leave out details.

This is the opposite of what the victimized partner needs. They want to know that it's on your mind all the time—that you haven't forgotten what you did and how much it hurt them. The clinical psychologist Janis Abrahms Spring, in her useful book *How Can I Forgive You?*, highlights how the more you focus on what you did, the less your partner has to: "You, the offender, demonstrate that you're fully conscious of your transgression and intend never to repeat it. You, the hurt party, become less preoccupied with the injury and begin to let it go."[5]

So you need to override your protectors, frequently bring up the incident and your remorse about it, and discuss how you are working with your parts to prevent a repeat. You also need to be patient with your partner's increased protectiveness. They may need to stay distant and hostile, suspicious and interrogative, for a long time until you have earned back their trust. Each time you criticize them for these behaviors, you set the process back.

As they see that you take seriously what you did and are working hard to change, they can relax their external vigilance enough to reconnect with their exiles that were so devastated by you. As your partner convinces the parts to trust them again as their primary caretaker, they can unburden the pain of your betrayal. It is at that point that genuine forgiveness is possible. Trying to forgive before that healing has occurred creates a forced forgiveness that winds up exiling the parts that are still distrusting and hurt.

When couples are able to repair and learn from big and small ruptures, they start to relax into the relationship. There is a feeling of movement—a sense that you won't remain stuck in the same old patterns for the rest of your lives. Most people find that they can tolerate many of their partner's quirks and irritations if they know they are temporary. It's when you feel as though you're stuck with all of that for the rest of your life that you get desperate. When both partners see the other commit to doing their work, they feel hopeful, and the obstacles that loomed so large shrink in the light of that hope. It was the deathless chronicity of the patterns that made them so intolerable.

Freed from the endless cycle of hurt, hollow promises, and disappointments, protectors gradually drop their weapons and increasingly shift from the anti group, described earlier, to the pro group. As their negative override becomes positive, partners become more accepting of each other's flaws, less reactive to each other's protectors, and more interested in making repairs after ruptures. In this safer environment, both partners can acknowledge and begin to heal their exiles. As they each become the primary caretaker of their unburdened exiles, they feel even less pressure to get the other to change, which paradoxically creates more space for the other to do so.

The Intimate Relationship

When this positive feedback loop takes root, you become very interested in your partner's inner discoveries and feel supportive of the work they're doing while also being fascinated by your own. Now the two of you are intimate companions supporting each other through external and internal journeys of growth and learning. You know that you will trigger each other, but you also know that you will repair and reconnect. All parts are welcome because no matter how extreme their initial presentation, you each know they are just parts and that once they tell their stories and unburden, they will reveal their value and be welcomed into your two-person collective inner family.

When couples really get this, they stop overreacting to each other's mood swings. When one partner has a "parts attack," the other stays Self-led and can encourage the triggered partner to help their part. This breaks the vicious cycle of parts wars that characterizes most distressed couples' interactions.

CHAPTER SIX

The Whole Picture

In this book, I've introduced such a large number of concepts and methods that it may be hard to picture how they fit together as a way of life. In this chapter, I will paint one picture of how it might work, with the caveat that it is necessarily simplified and may not fit your scenario completely. I will also explore intimacy in greater depth, describing four forms that it can take.

CONFLICT

If you fully hold the orientation of this book, the first difference you will notice is in your perspective. For example, you will no longer expect your partner to make you feel complete, worthwhile, elated, or safe—in other words, to be the primary caretaker of your parts. While your partner may elicit all of those feelings in you at different times, you know that you can help your parts feel that way, too, so their welfare doesn't depend on your partner. Then, when you don't feel those positive emotions, you don't blame your partner, and you don't give your partner all the credit when you do feel them.

Similarly, when you feel bereft, lonely, worthless, depressed, terrified, or humiliated, you don't depend totally on your partner to pull you out of those dark seas. You also don't grasp at the other life preservers our culture offers because you know how to turn to and love those hurting exiles. Or when your parts are so triggered that you can't help them in the moment, you hold the awareness that it is just a "parts attack" and is temporary. You have the ability to remain the "I" in the inner storm, which also helps you stay the "I" in outer storms with your partner. Once the storm blows over and the part calms down, you go with love to the ones that were upset and help them heal.

Similarly, you don't expect your partner to always maintain Self-leadership and, when they don't, you understand that it's just a "parts attack." When this is the case, you can keep your parts from overreacting if your partner is weak, needy, critical of you, enraged, scared, or distant. You remind your parts that it's just a small part of them that is probably young and reacting to some intense pain inside that you may or may not be the cause of; they don't necessarily mean all the extreme things that the part is saying, and you don't have to take personally or respond to the exaggerations in content. Instead, you sense the pain, shame, or fear that drives the part, and you respond with compassion; their Self is still in there despite the part, they are showing you, and it will return soon.

I can't always hold Self-leadership that way with an intimate partner, but when I can, it's an amazing experience. The same things she used to say that would explode in my gut and create emotional flooding, automatic retaliation, or withdrawal (which only fueled her parts' extremes) lose their power over me. Instead, I am often able to observe when her parts are activated and begin to make distortions and demands, with an understanding that she is speaking from a part that is likely very young and that is hurting deeply in these moments. I am often able to open to compassion and become interested in what the hurt is about, and I remind my parts that I don't have to meet her energy or counter the distortions. I reassure my parts that if they just let me stay and keep my heart open and my mind curious, she'll eventually come back. I also remind them that if it becomes clear that I have done something hurtful, that doesn't mean that I am bad, that she'll abandon me, or that I have to suffer. It simply means I need to make a repair.

The amazing thing is that she does come back—and often pretty quickly. Then we can bypass the fight followed by the hours or days of distance until one of us blinks. I don't have to listen internally to my parts rail ceaselessly about how unfair she is or how I should leave the relationship. Similarly, I avoid the lightning bolts of fear that now I've done it and she's going to leave me or hate me forever, or the pulses of shame that I'm such a failure as a partner. Neither of our protectors have to adopt one of the three projects. Instead, once she returns, we initiate a small repair session of a few minutes in which I say I'm sorry for the hurtful thing I did that triggered her part, and she says she's sorry that her part took over in such an extreme way. Bingo! We're connected again.

It is important to remember, however, that your ability to remain the "I" in the storm is strongly related to your ability to be the primary caretaker of your own parts. Before my parts trusted that I could care for them no matter what happened with her, I could never have resisted automatically reacting to her. The stakes were too high—her words were like knives piercing the hearts of my little exiles because they were so desperately attached to getting her love. My protectors had no choice but to counterattack or to put up walls. Once my parts came to trust me, those knives became blunted and bounced off their little bodies. Now I can have courageous love for her. When I stay the "I" in the storm, it's not to get her to change; instead, it's in keeping with the practice of fostering trust in my own Self-leadership.

The other shift in perspective that is crucial regarding these episodes of couples conflict is away from the ever-loving soul mate concept to the idea of partner as valuable tor-mentor. In the past, when my partner did something bothersome, I'd wonder, *Why am I stuck with someone who does things like that? Why can't she always be affectionate/considerate/sophisticated/ unselfish . . . ?* Now, perhaps after listening to some of that inner kvetching, I catch myself and shift focus away from her and toward what is hurting in me. There, hidden behind the kvetchers, I always find a part that needs my love and has not yet had a chance to unburden.

There will be times, of course, when there is no "I" in the storm—when both partners are so hijacked that neither can hold Self-leadership. Here again, expectations are crucial. When that used to happen to me, during the hijacking I would say to myself, *Clearly she doesn't love me, and I don't feel any love for her, so why are we together?* These fights would become the dark nights of our relationship because we would both take to heart the hurtful things we said to each other, and we didn't know how to initiate a repair afterward. As a result, they would produce more attachment reinjuries in both of us and would shift more parts of each other to the anti-relationship side. The resultant negative override would make each of us react to smaller things, creating more of the same.

Now when that mutual hijacking occurs, even if I can't stop my part from being extreme, I can remember that it's just a part and that the same is true of hers. With that knowledge, I remind myself that what gets said doesn't reflect our real feelings—that it's temporary and will be over soon and that we will repair and reconnect. It's as if I'm holding and reassuring the parts of me that get so scared by our protectors while they are warring. This inner reassurance minimizes the attachment reinjuries and anti-relationship stampede. I also expect that she and I will each use the fight to discover and heal the parts involved. With this set of under-standings and expectations, fights, while not exactly welcomed, are not dreaded and are viewed as valuable trailhead generators that will serve the future of our relationship.

I'll summarize this process around conflict below. First let's examine the new perspective that makes the difference:

> The fact that our partner triggers us is not a bad thing—we are here to learn lessons, and our partner is a great tor-mentor.

> When either of us is upset and extreme, it is just temporary hijacking by a part; our loving Selves are still in there and will return soon.

> The hijacking is useful because it will lead each of us to heal key exiles that are driving the protectors, if we follow through.

> Neither of us has to react in kind and can instead remain the "I" in the storm in the face of the other's hijacking.

> If both of us are hijacked, we can comfort our own exiles, even during the dark times.

It is our individual responsibility to be the primary caretaker of our own parts, and we can do that no matter what our partner does.

It is also our responsibility, later, to initiate a repair and to apologize for the parts of us that were extreme, regardless of what our partner did.

When you fully absorb this perspective, you can go through the following steps when your partner gets triggered and is hijacked by a protector:

Try not to overreact internally; remind your parts that you're still there with them and that there's pain behind her rage.

Either remain the "I" in the storm, or when you can't and your own protectors hijack as well, separate from them enough to know it's a parts attack and not your true feelings.

Later, do a U-turn—get curious about what was happening inside you during the episode, go inside to find out, and invite your partner to do the same.

Once you each discover the parts involved, disclose that information—especially the exiles that were driving the protectiveness—to the other as part of the repair.

Apologize for the extremes and commit to working with the parts you found.

Do that inner work when you have a chance and tell your partner about it later.

INTIMACY

Four Forms of Intimacy

That last step of telling your partner about your inner discoveries and healing leads us again to the topic of creating and maintaining intimacy. In my opinion, a primary aspect of intimacy involves knowing that you can reveal any part of yourself to your partner and trusting that you will eventually receive that person's love and acceptance in return. Toward the end of their therapy with me, Kevin and Helen Brady were beginning to experience the joy, relief, and sense of belonging that come from getting to know and accept each other so deeply.

It isn't easy to reach that level of intimacy because you are certain that so many parts of you are unacceptable and, as we discussed in the section on neo-exiles, because you believe that parts of you will threaten or repulse most partners. It takes a great deal of what I'm calling courageous love to listen to your partner tell you, for example, that they have a part that wants to have an affair or can't stand the way you look, and not freak out. It helps, however, if in telling you those things, your partner speaks for those parts rather than from them.

So much communication between couples is contained in the energy from which they speak. If you can speak from your Self, you can say even scary and challenging things, and, somewhere inside, your partner will hear your continued love for them. So, a second aspect of intimacy is the maintenance of an underlying Self-to-Self connectedness between you and your partner that provides a foundation for the risks you take with each other. This connection is built over time through the moments when the two of you drop your protectors and interact together in the calm, clear, confident, and courageous energy of Self. As they learned how to relate to each other from their Selves, Kevin and Helen were also building this kind of abiding sense of intimate connectedness.

There is a third aspect of intimacy that I have focused on less in this book because it may be most familiar to you already. It involves the connectedness that forms when each partner has a part that takes over and interacts with a similar or complementary part of the other. For example, some couples' primary connection comes from the interplay of their sexual parts. For others, it's from the playful banter of the ones that like to have fun and party. The intimacy of still other couples is produced by complementary connections, such as, for example, when one person's exile becomes attached to the other's protector or caretaker.

There is nothing wrong with this kind of intimacy per se, and when it occurs in the context of two Self-led, harmonious inner systems, it can be wonderful. But many couples' initial infatuation dance took place between two highly burdened parts whose need for each other overrode the better judgment of their two Selves. As was true for Kevin and Helen, some couples' unhealthy parts-based attachments are so powerful that they have to break them through separation before they can begin to care for their own exiles. Afterward, they can reunite and may find that those same part-to-part connections now are healthy adjuncts to their more complete closeness. Thus, part-to-part intimacy occurs best in a relationship that contains the other kinds as well.

The final form of intimacy is what I'll call the secondary caretaker kind. It is the bonding that occurs when one partner allows the other to be the secondary caretaker of their exiles. This Self-to-part connection across partners creates a loving gratitude in the receiver and a deep affection in the giver. When partners reach the stage when they can do this for each other, they fulfill the promise of relationship—to actively help each other learn the lessons about love and trust that we are all here to learn. They become true soul mates—not the kind of romantic fantasy but, instead, mates on the journey of the soul to discover how to give and receive love.

For example, after suffering in silence for a few days, Raul told Lupe that he had been hurt when she rejected his idea for a getaway weekend. As she listened with curiosity rather than defensiveness, he suddenly broke down and began weeping intensely. She moved quickly beside him, held his head to her chest, and gently asked, "What is it, baby? What's going on in there?" In a young, quivering voice, Raul said he was a loser and no one liked him. Lupe reassured him that that was not true for her and that she was sorry that other people had made him feel that way. After a few more minutes of comforting, Raul's exile receded. From his Self, Raul said he knew he had been feeling bad but didn't know it was coming from that boy who felt so worthless. He thanked Lupe for helping him find and reassure the boy and said he would take it from there. He also said that it was very scary to show that much weakness and to ask for what he wanted, so he was extremely grateful to Lupe for being so loving.

This kind of interaction between Lupe and Raul would have been impossible six months earlier because each of them held burdens around stereotypical gender roles that would have precluded it, and neither knew how to care for their own exiles. I encourage clients to wait until they are their exiles' primary caretaker before engaging in this form of intimacy because the odds are against it succeeding if they try it prematurely, and the consequences of failure are more attachment reinjuries. I also recommend that they wait until it can be mutual so as to avoid patterns in which one is always the parent and the other the child.

Each of these four forms of intimacy—describing parts to each other, Self-to-Self relating, part-to-part relating, and secondary caretaking (a.k.a. Self-to-part relating)—is powerful by itself. When all four are available in a relationship, it takes on a vitality that allows both partners to rest because they know they are home.

Each of these four forms of intimacy requires the ability to focus inside and express what you find. Too often, however, couples try to, or are encouraged by therapists to, achieve intimacy prematurely. There are some prerequisites to lasting intimacy that many couples and couples therapies ignore.

Prerequisites

The first prerequisite is time and energy. As we examined in the second chapter of this book, most couples today barely have time to coordinate their daily tasks, much less explore themselves and reveal what they find to each other. Intimacy is not for the exhausted, pressured, distracted, or overworked. If that describes you, and this predicament is truly unavoidable, adjust your expectations accordingly and wait until you have more peace and space in your life to actually get to know yourself and your partner. Don't blame your partner or yourself if you experience distance in your relationship—it can't be helped.

However, many people have protectors that convince them that such lifestyles are more necessary than they actually are. I have them work with those parts first, before we work on their relationship, to create enough space in their lives for them to have a chance for intimacy. So you may want to explore those striving, harried parts of you, as well as what they protect, before you try to achieve—or give up on—intimacy.

The second prerequisite is safety. Two of the four kinds of intimacy require high levels of vulnerability because you are exposing your exiles to your partner, which, for most people, is terrifying even in a very safe relationship. I don't encourage clients to give their partner direct access to their exiles until they trust that showing weakness or other intense, vulnerable emotions will not trigger their partner's distance, contempt, rejection, or other harsh protectors. For many couples, this will take time because they relate to their partner's exiles in the same way they do to their own. Until they change how they relate to their own exiles, it will be very hard not to punish their partner's.

The first two kinds of intimacy require less vulnerability and can be used to create safety. For example, you can tell your partner, as your Self, that you have a scared part that is afraid of their angry explosions. In doing so, you are far less vulnerable than when you become that young, fearful child in their presence who cries or shakes, and you are less likely to create a backlash reaction in them. I find that holding both partners in Self-leadership so they are speaking Self to Self and disclosing about—but not exposing—their parts can begin to create more safety. In other words, the first two kinds of intimacy can pave the way for the last two.

The most effective safety measure, however, is to help each partner become their own exiles' primary caretaker. When exiles in each partner are unburdened and are trusting their Selves, those young parts become less easily hurt by what the other does and more responsive to repair attempts. This inner reparenting may not be possible, however, in situations in which a client is constantly bombarded by a partner's scary or demeaning protectors. To create enough safety in such cases, couples may need to separate.

When these prerequisites are in place and couples begin to experience one or more of the four kinds of intimacy, they often say that this is all they've ever wanted. It turns out that our needs are pretty simple: to be seen and embraced, and to see and embrace. When we can clear away enough of the jungle to do that, we find a partner for life whose goal is to support our mutual learning and unburdening. With that blessing comes the joy of knowing we are doing what we are here to do, and we are not doing it alone.

GOOD LUCK

Like aging, intimate relationships should be experienced with openness and care. They require the courage to face what is ugly and scary in yourself and your partner, love fully without possessing, and risk losing that love. That is why intimate relationships are so rare—why so many people settle for protector-dominated lives together or choose to live alone. I have introduced a raft of provocative concepts and suggestions in this book whose unorthodox nature may make your head spin at first. All I can tell you is that they have served my clients and me extremely well. They vastly increase the odds that the risks you take for intimacy will lead to growth and healing. Happy trailheads, and may the Self be with you.

Resources

Anderson, Frank G. *Transcending Trauma: Healing Complex PTSD with Internal Family Systems*. Eau Claire, WI: PESI Publishing, 2021.

Anderson, Frank G., Martha Sweezy, and Richard C. Schwartz. *Internal Family Systems Skills Training Manual: Trauma-Informed Treatment for Anxiety, Depression, PTSD & Substance Abuse*. Eau Claire, WI: PESI Publishing, 2017.

Goulding, Regina A., and Richard C. Schwartz. *The Mosaic Mind: Empowering the Tormented Selves of Child Abuse Survivors*. Oak Park, IL: Trailheads, 1995.

Herbine-Blank, Toni, Donna M. Kerpelman, and Martha Sweezy. *Intimacy from the Inside Out: Courage and Compassion in Couple Therapy*. London: Routledge, 2015.

Herbine-Blank, Toni, and Martha Sweezy. *Internal Family Systems Couples Therapy Skills Manual: Healing Relationships with Intimacy from the Inside Out*. Eau Claire, WI: PESI Publishing, 2021.

McConnell, Susan. *Somatic Internal Family Systems Therapy: Awareness, Breath, Resonance, Movement and Touch in Practice*. Berkeley, CA: North Atlantic Books, 2020.

Schwartz, Richard C. *No Bad Parts: Healing Trauma and Restoring Wholeness with the Internal Family Systems Model*. Boulder, CO: Sounds True, 2021.

Schwartz, Richard C., and Robert R. Falconer. *Many Minds, One Self: Evidence for a Radical Shift in Paradigm*. Oak Park, IL: Trailheads, 2017.

Schwartz, Richard C., and Martha Sweezy. *Internal Family Systems Therapy.* 2nd ed. New York: Guildford Press, 2020.

Sweezy, Martha, and Ellen L. Ziskind. *Internal Family Systems Therapy: New Dimensions.* New York: Routledge, 2013.

Sweezy, Martha, and Ellen L. Ziskind. *Innovations and Elaborations in Internal Family Systems Therapy.* New York: Routledge, 2017.

Notes

Introduction

1. Debbie Ford, *The Secret of the Shadow: The Power of Owning Your Whole Story* (New York: HarperCollins, 2002), 3.
2. Ford, *Secret of the Shadow*, 3.
3. Ford, 5.
4. Ford, 6.
5. Richard C. Schwartz, *Internal Family Systems Therapy* (New York: Guilford Press, 1995); Richard C. Schwartz, *Introduction to Internal Family Systems* (Boulder, CO: Sounds True, 2023).
6. Walt Whitman, "Song of Myself," sec. 51, Poets.org, accessed September 25, 2022, poets.org/poem/song-myself-51.

Chapter One: Cultural Constraints to Intimacy

1. Margaret Mead, "Can Marriage Be for Life," in *Male and Female: A Study of the Sexes in a Changing World* (New York: HarperCollins, 2001). Originally published in 1949.
2. John Updike, "How to Love America and Leave It at the Same Time," *New Yorker*, August 11, 1972.
3. Leonard Cohen, "Stories of the Street," track 8 on *Songs of Leonard Cohen*, Columbia, 1967.
4. Philip Cushman, *Constructing the Self, Constructing America: A Cultural History of Psychotherapy* (New York: Addison Wesley, 1995).
5. Peter Walsh, *It's All Too Much: An Easy Plan for Living a Richer Life with Less Stuff* (New York: Free Press, 2007), 28.
6. Walsh, *It's All Too Much*, 79.

7. John F. Schumaker, *In Search of Happiness: Understanding an Endangered State of Mind* (London: Penguin, 2006), 228.
8. Frank Martela, Bent Greve, Bo Rothstein, and Juho Saari, "The Nordic Exceptionalism: What Explains Why the Nordic Countries Are Constantly Among the Happiest in the World," *World Happiness Report 2020,* March 20, 2020, worldhappiness.report/ed/2020/the-nordic-exceptionalism-what-explains-why-the-nordic-countries-are-constantly-among-the-happiest-in-the-world/.
9. Terrence Real, *I Don't Want to Talk About It: Overcoming the Secret Legacy of Male Depression* (New York: Fireside, 1997), 328.
10. John Gottman, *Why Marriages Succeed or Fail: What You Can Learn from the Breakthrough Research to Make Your Marriage Last* (New York: Simon & Schuster, 1994).
11. Gottman, *Why Marriages Succeed or Fail,* 147.

Chapter Two: The Development and Power of Exiles

1. Don Miguel Ruiz, *The Mastery of Love: A Practical Guide to the Art of Relationship* (San Rafael, CA: Amber-Allen, 1999).
2. Elizabeth Gilbert, *Eat, Pray, Love: One Woman's Search for Everything Across Italy, India, and Indonesia* (London: Penguin, 2006), 21.
3. Gilbert, *Eat, Pray, Love,* 20–21.
4. Mona Barbera, *Bring Yourself to Love: How Couples Can Turn Disconnection into Intimacy* (Boston: Dos Monos Press, 2008), xxii.
5. Barbera, *Bring Yourself to Love,* xxiii.

Chapter Three: Courageous Love and Doomed Relationships

1. Michael Ventura, *Shadow Dancing in the USA* (New York: St. Martin's Press, 1985), 19.
2. John Welwood, ed., *Challenge of the Heart: Love, Sex, and Intimacy in Changing Times* (Boston: Shambhala, 1985), 37.

3. Laura Kipnis, *Against Love: A Polemic* (New York: Pantheon, 2003), 3.
4. Welwood, *Challenge of the Heart*, 146.
5. Welwood, 158.
6. John M. Gottman, *The Seven Principles for Making Marriage Work: A Practical Guide from the Country's Foremost Relationship Expert* (New York: Three Rivers Press, 1999).
7. Gottman, *Seven Principles for Making Marriage Work*.
8. Mona Barbera, *Bring Yourself to Love: How Couples Can Turn Disconnection into Intimacy* (Boston: Dos Monos Press, 2008), x.

Chapter Four: An Example of Growing Toward Self-Leadership

1. Ernest Becker, *The Denial of Death* (New York: Simon & Schuster, 1977), 27.
2. Leonard Cohen, "Anthem," track 5 on *The Future*, Columbia, 1992.
3. Thomas Merton, *Seasons of Celebration: Meditations on the Cycle of Liturgical Feasts* (New York: Farrar, Straus and Giroux, 1965), 114–15.
4. John Welwood, *Love and Awakening: Discovering the Sacred Path of Intimate Relationship* (New York: HarperCollins, 1996), 231.
5. Pema Chödrön, *Start Where You Are: A Guide to Compassionate Living* (Boston: Shambhala, 1994), 56, 90.
6. Gregg Levoy, *Callings: Finding and Following an Authentic Life* (New York: Three Rivers Press, 1997), 180.

Chapter Five: Getting Practical: How to Bring In Courageous Love

1. Lydia Davis, *Almost No Memory: Stories* (New York: Farrar, Straus and Giroux, 1997), 82.
2. Terrence Real, *How Can I Get Through to You? Closing the Intimacy Gap Between Men and Women* (New York: Fireside, 2002), 243.
3. Real, *How Can I Get Through to You?*, 243–44.

4. Real, 244.

5. Janis Abrahms Spring, *How Can I Forgive You? The Courage to Forgive, the Freedom Not To* (New York: Perennial Currents, 2004), 124.

Bibliography

Barbera, Mona. *Bring Yourself to Love: How Couples Can Turn Disconnection into Intimacy*. Boston: Dos Monos Press, 2008.

Chödrön, Pema. *Start Where You Are: A Guide to Compassionate Living*. Boston: Shambhala, 1994.

Cushman, Philip. *Constructing the Self, Constructing America: A Cultural History of Psychotherapy*. New York: Addison Wesley, 1995.

Davis, Lydia. *Almost No Memory: Stories*. New York: Farrar, Straus and Giroux, 1997.

Ford, Debbie. *The Secret of the Shadow: The Power of Owning Your Whole Story*. New York: HarperCollins, 2002.

Gilbert, Elizabeth. *Eat, Pray, Love: One Woman's Search for Everything Across Italy, India, and Indonesia*. London: Penguin, 2006.

Gottman, John M. *The Seven Principles for Making Marriage Work: A Practical Guide from the Country's Foremost Relationship Expert*. New York: Three Rivers Press, 1999.

Gottman, John. *Why Marriages Succeed or Fail: What You Can Learn from the Breakthrough Research to Make Your Marriage Last*. New York: Simon & Schuster, 1994.

Kipnis, Laura. *Against Love: A Polemic*. New York: Pantheon, 2003.

Levoy, Gregg. *Callings: Finding and Following an Authentic Life*. New York: Three Rivers Press, 1997.

Merton, Thomas. *Seasons of Celebration: Meditations on the Cycle of Liturgical Feasts*. New York: Farrar, Straus and Giroux, 1965.

Real, Terrence. *How Can I Get Through to You? Closing the Intimacy Gap Between Men and Women.* New York: Fireside, 2002.

Real, Terrence. *I Don't Want to Talk About It: Overcoming the Secret Legacy of Male Depression.* New York: Fireside, 1997.

Ruiz, Don Miguel. *The Mastery of Love: A Practical Guide to the Art of Relationship.* San Rafael, CA: Amber-Allen, 1999.

Schumaker, John F. *In Search of Happiness: Understanding an Endangered State of Mind.* London: Penguin, 2006.

Schwartz, Richard C. "Don't Look Back." *Family Therapy Networker* (March/April 1997): 40–45.

Schwartz, Richard C. *Internal Family Systems Therapy.* New York: Guilford Press, 1995.

Schwartz, Richard C. *Introduction to Internal Family Systems.* Boulder, CO: Sounds True, 2023.

Spring, Janice Abrahms. *How Can I Forgive You? The Courage to Forgive, the Freedom Not To.* New York: Perennial Currents, 2004.

Ventura, Michael. *Shadow Dancing in the USA.* New York: St. Martin's Press, 1985.

Walcott, Derek. *Collected Poems, 1948–1984.* New York: Farrar, Straus and Giroux, 2007.

Welwood, John, ed. *Challenge of the Heart: Love, Sex, and Intimacy in Changing Times.* Boston: Shambhala, 1985.

Welwood, John. *Love and Awakening: Discovering the Sacred Path of Intimate Relationship.* New York: HarperCollins, 1996.

About the Author

Richard C. Schwartz, PhD, is the creator of Internal Family Systems, a highly effective, evidence-based therapeutic model that de-pathologizes the multipart personality. His IFS Institute offers training for professionals and the general public. He is currently on the faculty of Harvard Medical School and has published five books, including *No Bad Parts: Healing Trauma and Restoring Wholeness with the Internal Family Systems Model*. For more, visit ifs-institute.com.

About Sounds True

Sounds True is a multimedia publisher whose mission is to inspire and support personal transformation and spiritual awakening. Founded in 1985 and located in Boulder, Colorado, we work with many of the leading spiritual teachers, thinkers, healers, and visionary artists of our time. We strive with every title to preserve the essential "living wisdom" of the author or artist. It is our goal to create products that not only provide information to a reader or listener but also embody the quality of a wisdom transmission.

For those seeking genuine transformation, Sounds True is your trusted partner. At SoundsTrue.com you will find a wealth of free resources to support your journey, including exclusive weekly audio interviews, free downloads, interactive learning tools, and other special savings on all our titles.

To learn more, please visit SoundsTrue.com/freegifts or call us toll-free at 800.333.9185.

sounds true
WAKING UP THE WORLD